what works for
young adults

Am I depressed? What's wrong
college or career should I pursue? Enter
's wrong with America? Sex—how far is
religion is best? How can I be happy?
have to go to church? Why is the Bible b
okay to be single? Why am I depressed?
can I find peace? What's wrong with A
is Jesus really? What religion is best?
en is "good" good enough? Who is Jesus
y is the Bible boring? Do I have to go to
w can I be happy? What college or caree
how far is "too" far? How can I find

what works for
young adults
SOLID CHOICES IN UNSTABLE TIMES

Shane Idleman

What Works for Young Adults

Copyright © 2007 by Shane Idleman

E.P.
El Paseo
Publications

Published by El Paseo Publications
www.elpaseopublications.com

Cover design by Eric Rasmussen & Eric Walljasper
Interior design by Sandi Welch

All biblical references, unless specified otherwise, were obtained from the New King James version of the Bible published by Thomas Nelson, 1995.

Verses marked NIV are taken from the Holy Bible: New International Version ®. NIV ®. Copyright © 1973, 1978, 1984 by the International Bible Society. Verses marked NLT are taken from the New Living Translation. Copyright © 1996 by Tyndale Charitable Trust.

We make every effort to attribute the source of a quote to the correct author. If there is no acknowledgement, the author either wrote the quote or we could not determine the source. Not all quotes are referenced in the endnotes if the exact source could not be verified.

ISBN-13: 978-0-9713393-4-7
ISBN-10: 0-9713393-4-1

Library of Congress Control Number: 2006907667

Printed in the United States of America
10 9 8 7 6 5 4 3 2 1

"Sit down, buckle up, and hold on! This is one of the best resources for young adults in the publishing industry today."

—TIM WILDMON; PRESIDENT, American Family Association.

"*What Works for Young Adults* is a book whose message every young person would do well to ponder carefully."

—D. JAMES KENNEDY, PH.D.; Coral Ridge Ministries; Ft. Lauderdale, FL.

"*What Works for Young Adults* challenges, encourages, and inspires young adults to live a life guided by integrity not popularity. Shane continually points to the fact that no other decision will impact the lives of young adults more than who, or what they choose to follow. A must read for all ages!"

—TONY PERKINS; President, Family Research Council; Washington, D.C.

"If you're comfortable struggling with the same old issues … this is not a book for you, but if you're tired of spiritual compromise … make it a point to read and apply the principles presented in this book."

—PASTOR BOB COY; Calvary Chapel of Ft. Lauderdale, FL.

"We are told that approximately 76-million Americans were born from 1982 to 2000; they are known as the 'Millennials.' These young adults need spiritual guidance and direction. Shane Idleman has hit the nail on the head. *What Works for Young Adults* can help an entire generation find God. This is a must read!"

—DR. MIKE MACINTOSH; Pastor of Horizon Christian Fellowship; San Diego, CA.

"When I read Shane Idleman, Jesus's words from Matthew 11:19 come to mind: 'Wisdom is proved right by her actions.' Shane creatively, clearly and powerfully offers wisdom that's not only practical, but that also goes straight to the heart. With insights from the Scriptures, from great Christian writers, as well as from our founding fathers and historic leaders, young adults (and not so young adults!) will here find what works when things aren't working right."

—PETER LILLBACK; President, The Providence Forum and Senior Pastor, Proclamation Presbyterian Church.

TABLE OF CONTENTS

The *What Works* Book Series
BOOK #4

EL PASEO PUBLICATIONS IS COMMITTED TO QUALITY in publication—to inspire, educate, and encourage the highest standard of excellence through written communication. Other books by the author include: *What Works When "Diets" Don't, What Works for Singles—for Relationships, for Marriage, for Life,* and *What Works for Men—Regaining Lost Ground.*

Scriptures and quotes within "quotation marks" are exact quotes; whereas, paraphrased Scriptures and quotes are often italicized. In some cases, only portions of Scriptures are referenced. The Bible is the ultimate authority; all Scriptures should be read in their complete context whenever possible.

This book seeks to identify the middle ground between our responsibility and God's role in changing us. We have responsibilities, yet we are totally dependent on God. We must do our part, but we can't do His. *It is God who makes us stand firm in Christ* (II Corinthians 1:21). Seek Him.

ACKNOWLEDGMENTS

by Shane Idleman

WANT TO THANK MY WIFE, MORGAN, AND MY DAUGHTER, Aubrey; both have been a tremendous blessing. Their unconditional love provides stability and strength through ongoing challenges. Thank you, Morgan, for the additional insight and editing, and for believing in me and in the *What Works Book Series*—your continued encouragement is truly a blessing. Thank you Aubrey for being the best daughter that a father could ask for.

I also want to thank my mother, Diane Idleman, who has continued to offer guidance and encouragement. Not only is she a great mother, but an exceptional editor and "book doctor." She provided the editorial overview of this book as well as the others. The Book Series would not be what it is today had it not been for her insight. Thank you for the many days, nights, weeks, and months invested—may it return a hundred-fold. Aside from the Lord, in the words of Abraham Lincoln, *all that I am, and all that I'll ever be, I owe to my mother.*

A special thanks to my brother, Ryan, and his wife, Christina, along with Christian and Austin, as well as my sister Meredith, her husband, Chris, and their son, Hayden— all have been a tremendous blessing. I thank God for family members who add to life rather than take from it.

I also want to thank Morgan's family for their support and acceptance: Augie, Linda, and Curt, as well as Leah, Shawn, Jessica, Allison, and Kelsey.

I also want to acknowledge my father, Jim Idleman, who died of a heart attack in his early fifties. He inspired me more than he could have known. Qualities such as honesty, integrity, commitment, discipline, and a very strong work ethic are not easily taught. Values are not transmitted through mere words; they are instilled through a life that models these traits. I'll be forever grateful for the experiences we shared, the lessons I learned, and the man that I became as a result of the time that we spent together.

Additional appreciation is offered to those who provided cover quotes, and to my pastors, friends, and church leaders for their support, encouragement, comments, and suggestions, including Pastors Sean Appleton, Chris Johnson, Mike Morris, and Bryan Sederwall, as well as Professor Mike McCormick, and Justin T. Alfred—*Word in Life Ministries*. Thank you for taking the time to thoroughly review the manuscript and/or offer feedback; it was greatly appreciated.

Finally, special thanks to the focus groups and individuals who offered great suggestions: Michael, Byron, Verity, Cathy, Steven, Kelli, Challen, Cindy, Cassandra, Josh, Ricardo, Yolanda, Heather, Brad and everyone that I may have missed, as well as the entire Engel and Lonergan family.

A note of recognition—past and present

PRESENT: Although unaware of their influence, several Christian leaders have contributed to my spiritual development throughout the years. A special thanks to David Barton, Alistair Begg, James Dobson, Billy and Franklin Graham, Jack Hayford, Tommy Jakes, David Jeremiah, D. James Kennedy, John MacArthur, James MacDonald, J.I.

Packer, Paul E. Sheppard, Chuck Smith, Charles Stanley, Chuck Swindoll, and Ravi Zacharias, to name only a few.

PAST: The following men are no longer with us; however, their legacies continue to live. They have not only been an incredible inspiration to me, but to countless others as well—a special note of appreciation to the following:

- *Jonathan Edwards* (1703-1758), minister and theologian who contributed greatly to the Great Awakening—a spiritual movement in America in the 1730s and 1740s that breathed new spiritual life into the Colonies.

- *John Wesley* (1703-1791), founder of Methodism and a key figure in the Great Awakening.

- *George Whitefield* (1714-1770), primary evangelist during the Great Awakening.

- *Charles Haddon Spurgeon* (1834-1892), considered one of the best preachers of the nineteenth century.

- *D. L. Moody* (1837-1899), one of the greatest evangelists of all time.

- *Oswald Chambers* (1874-1917), a gifted teacher, author, and minister who wrote the devotional classic, *My Utmost for His Highest.*

- *A.W. Tozer* (1897-1963), a bold Christian Missionary Alliance minister who authored several inspiring books.

- *Martin Luther King, Jr.* (1929-1968), Christian leader and recognized Founder of the Civil Rights Movement.

- *D. Martyn Lloyd-Jones* (1899-1981), a theologian, as well as a powerful Welsh preacher.

- *Adrian Rogers* (1931-2005), pastor of Belleview Baptist Church in Memphis, Tennessee, for 33 years. His character and ministry inspired evangelicals worldwide.

Many are willing to go in God's direction, but only if He's going in theirs.

———————

No other decision will impact your life more than who or what you choose to follow.

CHAPTER ONE

GOD? Truth?

Guardrails

IF YOU HAVEN'T NOTICED, many challenging issues arise during the young adult years. If you've ever needed solid answers, it's now.

Before we move on, let's establish one fact: you were created for a purpose; your life has meaning. Regardless of how others have made you feel, God created you; you are not an accident. No matter what you've gone through, or are going through, **your past does not have to define your future.**

God's Word provides encouragement and direction as you face tough decisions; therefore, a large portion of this book draws from the Scriptures. Don't simply glance over Scripture references, even if you've read them before. Read them again to see how each relates to you today. Don't let the surplus of information and the biblical principles make you

God's principles are guardrails through the canyons of life. They don't prevent us from enjoying life; they protect us from falling.

feel that you cannot measure up. We all fall short, and we all have issues that we struggle with. Spiritual maturity takes time. One step in the right direction leads to another, and then another, and so on.

Finally, don't tackle these issues on your own; seek God's help and pray for guidance. *It's difficult to stumble when you're on your knees.*

Unfortunately, we often view the Bible only as a book of "DOs & DON'Ts," instead of a book that contains absolute truth. It guides, defends, and protects. God's principles are guardrails through the canyons of life. They don't prevent us from enjoying life; they protect us from falling. With that said, let's begin with the first topic—*absolute truth.*

Going in the wrong direction

I learned a lesson as a very young boy that still applies today. One summer, I was on an early morning bike ride to school. As I turned the corner and headed west, a heavy gust of wind slowed my pace. It was clear that I would be late for school, so I turned around and headed home for a ride. To my surprise, when I changed directions, my bike felt as if it were gliding on air. I turned and headed back to school, but once again, I was bombarded with gusts of wind that nearly blew me over.

At that young age I realized what had happened. The wind was against me as I headed in one direction, but with me as I headed in the other. Isn't that true so many times in life? One direction can be challenging and another effortless. In the same way, as you embrace "absolute truth," it may seem as though you are pushing against the flow of society, and often, you will be. But here's the principle: even though it was easier for me to go with the wind when I turned back, I was actually going in the wrong direction.

When it comes to believing in absolute truth, understand that there will be resistance. No resistance may mean that you are going in the wrong direction as well—it's often easier to go with the flow of society than against it. Martin Luther said, **"Where the battle rages, there the loyalty of the soldier is tested."**[1] A commitment to uphold absolute truth will result in resistance. Don't let this discourage you. In the same way that resistance training builds physical strength, spiritual opposition will strengthen your spiritual foundation.

As a young adult, I often went with the flow of society and focused on everything that the world had to offer. Throughout my 20s, I continued to run from God, searching for identity and truth in everything but His Word. By age 28, I was a corporate executive in Southern California. Money and success became my gods and ultimately controlled my life. I was driven, but for the wrong reasons. I felt a sense of purpose, but it often left me feeling empty. I was passionate, but for the wrong things. As a result of my misguided focus, my life took several unnecessary turns for the worse. By then, alcohol, anger, and arrogance had taken their toll.

Sometime later, still unfulfilled, depressed, and desperate for direction, I began to thumb through the pages of my

Bible that was shelved long ago. As I read, two Scriptures seemed to jump from the pages: *what does it profit you to gain the whole world but lose your soul?* (Luke 9:25), and, *when you hear God's voice do not harden your hearts against Him* (Psalm 95:7-8). I suddenly realized just how far I had drifted from the truth. I was at a turning point—I could choose to humble myself, regain lost ground, and follow God's absolute truth, or continue to reject it. By God's grace, I put my complete trust in Him. Joy, happiness, and peace filled my heart. Within the months that followed, my passion and purpose for life became clearer than ever. Psalm 32:8 gave me new hope, and it can give you hope as well: "I will instruct you and teach you in the way you should go; I will guide you with My eye." I may not have known where my steps were leading, but God did, and He radically changed my direction. He wants to lead you as well.

Isn't truth relative?

Many have accepted the notion that truth is relative to the circumstance; this is commonly known as *relativism*; a very popular and pervasive deception that runs throughout our culture—"every man doing whatever is right in his own eyes" (Deuteronomy 12:8).

This reminds me of a university professor who told his class that what was wrong for him might not be wrong for someone else. One student challenged him on this. Midway through his lecture, the student walked over to the professor's desk and pushed his paperwork on the floor. Extremely upset, the professor demanded an answer for the student's outrageous behavior. The student calmly replied, "What's wrong for you may not be wrong for me." From this simple illustration, you can see that *relativism* does not make sense.

There are certain "rights" and "wrongs" called absolutes that are given by God to save man from himself.

There are certain "rights" and "wrongs" called absolutes that are given by God to save man from himself. *God's Word is truth* (John 17:17).

As another example, can we drive recklessly without suffering any consequences? Of course not. There are certain "absolutes" that must be followed to prevent accidents. Can we show up for work whenever we like, or leave before the job is done? No, not if we want to keep our job. There are schedules, policies, and job descriptions that must be followed. Why then, when it comes to absolute spiritual truth, which is vastly more important, do we believe that we can pick and choose? If we apply only what we want, we can easily miss what we need.

My younger years provide another illustration. During the summer, my family took frequent trips to the Sierra Nevada Mountains in California. As independent as I was at 18 years old, I didn't question the wisdom of staying on the highways that led to my destination. Signs led; I followed. Similarly, the way has been clearly defined for you in God's Word—follow the directions and keep the course—detours will cost you. It's been said that *bad decisions take you farther than you want to go, cost you more than you want to pay, and keep you longer than you want to stay.* I couldn't agree more. **Without God leading the way, we wander aimlessly.**

Some argue that since we can't see, touch, taste, smell, or hear God, that He must not exist, but this is not true. When I worked in the construction industry, I attended a *Confined Space Training* class. This training was mandatory for anyone desiring to work in a confined or enclosed space, such as a vault or a tank. I was fascinated to learn that there are poisonous gases inside many confined spaces that can kill within seconds. The only way to detect them is with a special device. You can't see, touch, taste, smell, or hear the poisonous gas, but it's there, and so is God. Life-sustaining oxygen is also undetectable through our senses, as is our life-sustaining Creator. But "His invisible attributes are clearly seen." (Check out Romans 1:20.)

Sadly, many reject the Bible as absolute truth because absolute truth, by definition, is exclusive. They do not like exclusivity; they want the freedom, as did I, to do what they want, when they want, how they want, to whom they want. They're willing to go in God's direction, but only if He's going in theirs. As a result, many embrace the occult, horoscopes, spiritual advisors, witchcraft, New Age philosophy, or other things in search of truth. But God clearly warns against this in Isaiah 30:1, "Woe to the rebellious children, says the Lord, who take counsel, but not of Me, and who devise plans, but not of My Spirit." Isaiah, an Old Testament prophet, proclaimed God's Word at an important time in history. In this verse, God warned against looking to anything or anyone other than Him for the truth. Although Isaiah lived centuries ago, the same truth applies today: *truth is not relative.* No other decision will impact our lives more than who or what we choose to follow. For this reason, lay aside "feelings" and "opinions" as you search for absolute truth. **Feelings and opinions change—truth does not!**

For the time will come

Although disheartening, society's trend away from God's Word and absolute truth is not surprising. The apostle Paul warned of this many years ago: "For the time will come when they will not endure sound doctrine [God's Word], but according to their own desires ... they will turn their ears away from the truth, and be turned aside to fables" (II Timothy 4:3-4).

Searching for spiritual fulfillment isn't wrong, but where we search can be. There is tremendous power and wisdom in the Bible. Many religions and cults recognize its influence, often adding portions of the Bible to their own writings. In studying various religions, I learned that most originated from someone claiming to have received a "vision from God," a "new revelation," or a "deeper truth" that contradicts the Bible. These self-proclaimed prophets use their visions to begin their religion, and the rest is history. The fact that these groups have greatly altered the truth of God's Word is a startling reality. Who would you rather trust your soul to, God or man? **We don't change God's message—His message changes us.**

There are not "many" ways to God. The Bible and the beliefs of other religions cannot all be right. The Bible was not written "in addition to" anything; it stands alone. The apostle John, who walked with Jesus, said *to test everything* (I John 4:1), and Jesus said in Matthew 24:24 that *false Christs and false prophets will appear and deceive many.* A "prophet," as mentioned here, can be anyone in a position of spiritual authority, or claiming to be.

How do we "test every spirit" and avoid false teachers? It's actually very simple: determine if what they are teaching agrees with the Scriptures. For example, if a cult or religion

Unless a person is anchored in God's Word, knows what the Bible says, and believes it, *he or she will be like a child tossed back and forth and carried away by every wind of doctrine, by the trickery of men* **(Ephesians 4:14)**.

says that there are many gods, Isaiah 45:22 tells us otherwise: "For I am God, and there is no other." If they claim that a "messenger of light" appeared to one of their prophets as the voice of God, we should point them to II Corinthians 11:14 where "Satan himself transforms himself into an angel of light." If someone says that righteousness is only obtained by following rigid codes of financial and moral requirements, the New Testament says otherwise—we are saved by grace through faith in Jesus Christ. Can you see the unparalleled truth in all of this? Unless a person is anchored in God's Word, knows what the Bible says, and believes it, *he or she will be like a child tossed back and forth and carried away by every wind of doctrine, by the trickery of men* (Ephesians 4:14). It's vitally important that we study the Bible.

Satan counteracts truth through deceptions and counterfeits. A good example of this is the fabricated book and movie, *The Da Vinci Code*. It's been said that if as many Christians who read *The Da Vinci Code* had read their Bibles, America would have experienced a revival. Surprisingly, many who read this book actually believe it. This shouldn't catch us off guard, remember Paul's warning to Timothy, that *a time will come when people will not be receptive to God's Word. They will look for teachers who will tell them what they want to hear instead of what they need to hear. As a result, many will turn from the truth and begin to follow fables.* Galatians 1:8 adds, "But even if we [the writers of the Bible], or an angel from heaven, preach any other gospel to you than what we have preached to you, let him be accursed."

Cults take advantage of the fact that many people are not well educated in fundamental biblical truths. **To detect a counterfeit, one must first know what the original looks like.** It's impossible to gain a clear picture of absolute truth without going directly to God's Word. Unless one is firmly grounded in God's Word and led by His Spirit, one can easily be led astray.

This reminds me of a person that I once knew who experimented with different religions and read dozens of "spiritual" books. He rejected the Bible as absolute truth. As a result, he was confused, depressed, and uncertain about life; he lacked direction and purpose. I often reminded him that where he was looking was what he was finding. The same holds true with you and me. **We wouldn't look for fish in the Mojave Desert, or almonds on a palm tree, but**

❝ *There is a kind of truth which can never be grasped by the intellect, for the intellect exists for the apprehension of ideas, and this truth consists not in ideas but in life.* **❞**

—A.W. TOZER

that's exactly what we do when we look for truth outside of God's Word.

A.W. Tozer said, "There is a kind of truth which can never be grasped by the intellect, for the intellect exists for the apprehension of ideas, and this truth consists not in ideas but in life."[2] The human mind, apart from God's Spirit, will never comprehend or understand spiritual truth. I Corinthians 2:14 (NIV) validates this: "The man without the Spirit does

Man-made religions are lifeless; there's no spiritual life in them.

not accept the things that come from the Spirit of God, for they are foolishness to him, and he cannot understand them, because they are spiritually discerned." This is why many reject the Bible or change its message—their natural mind does not receive the things of God; truth is foolishness to them. What does this mean to you and to me? Everything. Man-made religions are lifeless; there's no spiritual life in them.

In my case, I realized that I had been looking for truth and fulfillment in all the wrong places. While I had focused on things such as money, status, physical appearance, and relationships, I had starved my soul. I found that before meaningful, lasting change can occur on the outside, it first must occur on the inside. We cannot successfully change actions or attitudes unless God changes our heart.

Reflecting back, I see that many of my wrong choices could have been prevented had I simply followed God's plan for my life and embraced His absolute truth. We cannot take from the Bible what we choose and disregard the rest. We must look to the Architect who created us and follow His plan as He designed it.

At this point, you may have countless questions; don't worry. Throughout the book, I continue to reference Scriptures that will answer some of those questions. Read the Scripture references for yourself, and in their entirety. This will lead to an even greater understanding of God's Word. It would be a waste of precious time not to allow God to direct your life through His Word. His Word is living and powerful. (Check out Hebrews 4:12.)

Enough cannot be said about the one, unquestionable proof that the Bible is the inspired Word of God. The greatest witness is a *transformed life*. Even Rousseau, the French skeptic, said: "I must confess to you that the majority of the Scriptures astonish me; the holiness of the evangelists speaks to my heart and has such striking characters of truth ... that if it had been the invention of men, the inventors would be greater than the greatest heroes."[3] Unfortunately, Rousseau was unwilling to replace preference with truth.

So now what?

First, find a Bible-based, Christ-centered church that passionately preaches the truth of God's Word. I'm frequently astonished at the number of people who no longer attend church because of a bad experience, dislike of the music, or some similar reason. Can you imagine if we applied that thought to everyday living? If we have a bad experience at a restaurant, should we never dine out again? If we have a bad experience with our car, should we never drive again? There are, however, some churches, groups, and people that should be avoided. The key is to compare what they're saying and doing with the Word of God. Also, look for characteristics such as encouragement, love, and support.

Second, devote a portion of your day (morning, noon, or night) to prayer and building intimacy with God; some refer to this as "quiet time." This time is vitally important. Although a few different translations are referenced in this book, I recommend that you obtain a good study Bible that is a *word-for-word* translation. (The *King James, New King James,* and *New American Standard* versions of the Bible are my choices.) I've heard that we should *read* the Bible to get God's perspective, *meditate* on it to get God's direction, *study* it to learn how to apply it, and *memorize* it to help us make the right decisions.

Thirdly, it's imperative that you develop relationships with those who will encourage you to grow in your faith. You may even consider listening online to some of the people in the Acknowledgments section of this book. Remember: what you put into your relationship with God is what you'll get out. That leads us to the next chapter—*Knowing God: religion vs. relationship.*

Questions to consider for Chapter One:

1. Do you agree that God's principles are guardrails through the canyons of life—they don't prevent us from enjoying life, they protect us from falling? If so, why are so many opposed to them?

2. Do you agree that there will be resistance when embracing absolute truth? How can this resistance help your spiritual growth?

3. Reflect on the verse: "Woe to the rebellious children, says the Lord, who take counsel, but not of Me, and who devise plans, but not of my Spirit" (Isaiah 30:1). What does it mean to you? Where do you look for counsel and truth?

4. Do you agree that searching for spiritual fulfillment isn't wrong, but where we search can be? Do you feel that the enemy tries to convince us that truth is relative and that we should follow our own desires? Why is this dangerous?

5. Comment on this statement: unless a belief is grounded in Scripture it cannot be trusted. Cults take advantage of the fact that many people are not well educated in fundamental biblical truths.

Recommended Reading:
The Kingdom of the Cults by Walter Martin
A Ready Defense by Josh McDowell
What If Jesus Had Never Been Born by D. James Kennedy
The Da Vinci Deception by Erwin W. Lutzer

Man's way leads to
a hopeless end—God's way
leads to an endless hope.

———————————

If your religion has not
changed your life,
change your religion.

CHAPTER TWO

KNOWING GOD
Religion vs. Relationship

Follow Me

WHEN I WAS A YOUNG MAN, I believed that I was strong because I could bench press over 400 pounds, drink a 12-pack of beer, and win most of the fights that I was in. What I failed to realize was that I was weak; I was dying spiritually. **I didn't have control of my life—my life had control of me.** Years later, I read again about the life of Jesus Christ, this time with open eyes. I found that I had been completely wrong about Him. Who, but Jesus, would say, *no man takes my life, I lay it down willingly?* Who, but Jesus, would say to the judge who ordered His execution, *you would have no power over me unless it was given to you from above?* Who, but Jesus, when hanging on a cross, severely beaten and dying for our sins, would say of his accusers, *Father, forgive them, for they*

> Weakness is the absence of strength; meekness is strength under control. It takes far more strength to follow Christ than to go with the flow of society.

know not what they do? (See John 10:18; John 19:11; and Luke 23:34.) Following Christ does not represent weakness; it represents meekness. Weakness is the absence of strength; meekness is strength under control. It takes far more strength to follow Christ than to go with the flow of society.

Two words from Jesus: "Follow Me"—have changed more lives than all the words of famous men combined. As the great preacher, Charles Haddon Spurgeon, once said: **"The grace that is not strong enough to change me will not be able to save me."** We don't need to be ashamed of Christ and what He did for us. The apostle Paul said: "For I am not ashamed of the gospel of Christ, for it is the power of God to salvation for everyone who believes" (Romans 1:16).

Why then are so many disturbed when the name of Jesus is mentioned? Why is His name, above all others, often taken in vain? The answer is simple: there is power in His name— power that shakes the spiritual realm. Philippians 2:9-11 says that *God has highly exalted Him and has given Him a name that is above every other name, that at the name of Jesus every knee will bow and every tongue will confess that Jesus Christ is Lord.* No wonder the enemy seeks to destroy our relationship with Jesus; it's the only name that can defeat him. Martin Luther said, "When Jesus Christ utters a word,

He opens His mouth so wide that it embraces all Heaven and earth, even though that word be but in a whisper."[4]

Is your current belief system producing assurance, purpose, and peace, or is it bringing discouragement, disappointment, and despair? Jesus said, **"Wisdom is shown to be right by what results from it"** (Matthew 11:19 NLT). Is your faith leading you in the right direction? If not, consider who or what is leading you—religious tradition, or a relationship with Jesus Christ. "There is no peace until we see the finished work of Jesus Christ—until we can look back and see the cross of Christ between our sins" (D.L. Moody).

> *Religion says,* "I have to follow rules." A relationship with Christ says, "Because of the price that He paid for me, I want to follow His plan for my life."

> *Religion says,* "I have to go to church." A relationship with Christ says, "I want to position myself to learn more, worship Him, and benefit from fellowship."

> *Religion lacks assurance;* a relationship with Jesus offers unfailing guidance and assurance.

> *Religion is man's attempt to reach God;* a relationship with Christ is God reaching down to man.

When people misunderstand and become dissatisfied and discouraged with Christianity, it's often because they confuse "religion" and "rules" with a true relationship with Christ. They base their opinion of Christianity on how they see other Christians act. This can be dangerous. Don't base your opinion of Christianity solely on the actions of others. **One of the greatest threats to Christianity is not in our failure to proclaim it, but in our inability to live it out.**

❝ Millions of professed believers talk as if [Christ] were real and act as if He were not. And always our actual position is to be discovered by the way we act, not by the way we talk. ❞

—A.W. TOZER

Why do many leave Sunday morning church services no different than when they arrived? In many cases, it's because they have religion and not a true relationship with Jesus. No wonder Jesus said that *many people draw near to Him with their words, but their hearts are far from Him* (Matthew 15:8). A.W. Tozer states it best: "Millions of professed believers talk as if [Christ] were real and act as if He were not. And always our actual position is to be discovered by the way we act, not by the way we talk."5

In the New Testament, Jesus had harsh words for those who appeared to be religious but inwardly had not changed. Our actions, not our words, reveal the authenticity of our relationship with Christ. I don't say this to promote a performance-based religion; I say it to demonstrate the importance of having a loyal, committed, genuine relationship with Jesus. In Matthew 7:13, Jesus commanded us *to enter by the narrow gate, as opposed to walking through the wide gate that leads to destruction.* Jesus was demonstrating the importance of having a personal relationship with Him, rather than following the crowd, religious tradition, or the latest fad.

Who is Jesus? How we answer this question is the difference between right and wrong, light and darkness, heaven and hell. When asked this question, the apostle Peter gave the correct response: "You are the Christ, the Son of the living God" (Matthew 16:16). Jesus Himself confirmed this by saying: "I am the way, the truth, and the life. No one comes to the Father except through Me" (John 14:6).

Seriously consider who and what you choose to follow. Man's way leads to a hopeless end—God's way leads to an endless hope. God has shown us the way, not through religion, but through a relationship.

It's all about 'Who' you know

We have faith in banks, businesses, vehicles, buildings, friends ... an endless list, but when it comes to having faith in an all-knowing and all-powerful God, we seem to have difficulty. Many find it hard to accept Jesus as the Son of God. They don't understand why God sent Him, if they believe at all. Ravi Zacharias, a leading apologist, said, "The denial of Christ has less to do with facts and more to do with the bent of what a person is prejudiced to conclude."[6] In other words, people often reject the Bible and a relationship with Jesus Christ not because they lack facts, but because they do not want to surrender their will and give up the so-called "good life"; they don't want there to be a God. It's often an issue of the heart, not the intellect.

We are sinners who need a Savior. Jesus came to seek and to save that which was lost. Hebrews 9:22 says that *without the shedding of blood, there is no removal of sin.* His blood was shed for our sins; we should be forever thankful. **Jesus isn't an option; He's the way, the truth, and the life** (John 14:6).

We hear a great deal about God's judgment and what can keep us from heaven, and rightly so, because "the fear of the Lord is the beginning of knowledge" (Proverbs 1:7). But we also need to reflect on God's goodness, love, mercy, and grace. *For God so loved the world that He gave His only Son, that whosoever believes in Him shall not perish but have everlasting life* (John 3:16). Take a minute and ponder that verse: God loved us so much that He allowed His Son to die on a cross for our sins. This alone should inspire us to follow Him.

It's difficult to transmit my love for Jesus on these pages. He healed my brokenness and restored my life, and he can do the same for you. If you only take one thing from this book, I hope that it is this: there is a deep longing inside all of us that cannot be satisfied until we recognize our need for a Savior and turn to Him.

If you feel that your relationship with Christ is not genuine, or if you've never repented and trusted in Him as your Lord and Savior, now is the time to take that step and fully commit your entire life. This is often referred to as being "born again." Romans 10:9 states that "if you confess with your mouth the Lord Jesus and believe in your heart that God has raised Him from the dead, you will be saved." (Check out John 3:1-21.)

Being "born again" is a spiritual rebirth, a true gift from God; it should affect everything in our lives. **If our priorities, our passions, our goals, our dreams, and our desires are not changing—are we changing?** I say this because so many today have religion, and not a true relationship with Christ; they're simply going through the motions. It's been said that if your religion has not changed your life, change your religion. Of course there are hobbies, activities, and certain friendships that will continue, but if our overall nature is not changing, or at least heading in

" *The gospel, when rightly understood and received, sets the heart against all sin.* **"**

—MATTHEW HENRY

that direction, we should reassess our commitment—was it genuine? Do we truly "know" Jesus Christ (relationship), or do we only know "about" Him (religion)?

"The gospel, when rightly understood and received, sets the heart against all sin" (Matthew Henry). A disobedient life should raise concerns. Tozer said it this way, "The idea that God will pardon a rebel who has not given up his rebellion is contrary both to the Scriptures and to common sense."[7] (See II Thessalonians 1:8.)

In William Martin's book, *A Prophet With Honor—The Billy Graham Story,* Mr. Martin wrote of young Billy's conversion at a revival service. Martin added that although Billy was a "mental storehouse of Scripture" and "vice-president of his church's youth group [before his conversion] ... he probably never imagined that he was not a Christian," but the sermon that he heard at the revival service convicted and convinced him that he had not yet fully surrendered his life to Christ—knowledge *about* Jesus was not enough.[8]

I John 2:3-4 says, "Now by this we know that we know Him, if we keep His commandments. He who says, 'I know Him [Christ],' and does not keep His commandments, is a liar, and the truth is not in him." The word "keep" here means *to keep watchful care of.* In the same way that a ship's captain is committed to keep his course to reach his destination, the sincerity of our commitment to Christ can be measured by how well we follow the scriptural course, with love as the guiding force. From time to time, we, like ships, will drift off course. **Perfection is not the answer; a commitment to keep the course is.** Keep the course by *loving the Lord your God with all your heart, soul, and mind; this is the greatest commandment* (Matthew 22:37-38).

If you're searching and not finding, hurting and not healing, and living but not loving, I encourage you to look to the One who has the answers and commit your life to Him. No matter what you have done or have experienced, from sexual abuse and abortion, to promiscuity and/or homosexuality, you have the ability to turn to Christ and start anew. One famous quote captures it well: "A true measure of a person is not who they were, but who they will become." It's all about Who you know!

When is 'good' good enough?

Did you know that doing "good works" will not save us? This is another distinction between religion and a relationship. **Religion focuses on what "we" do; a relationship with Christ focuses on what "He" did.** The mark of genuine faith is not found in religious involvement, visible acts of kindness, knowledge of Jesus,

Genuine faith is reflected in a transformed life, a love for God and His Word, sincere humility, selfless love, true repentance, and a disconnect from the world.

or even in the conviction of sin. Genuine faith is reflected in a transformed life, a love for God and His Word, sincere humility, selfless love, true repentance, and a disconnect from the world. I once heard Pastor Greg Laurie ask, "If you were arrested for being a Christian, is there enough evidence in your life to convict you?" Jesus said, "No one can serve two masters" (Matthew 6:24). It's been said that if Christ is not Lord of all, He's not Lord at all. Charles Spurgeon adds, **"We cannot follow two things. If Christ be one of them, we cannot follow another."** If He's not Lord, it may be because we have not yielded. Change occurs when there is a strong conviction of sin and genuine repentance. (Repentance is a change of mind that leads to a change of action.)

Jesus said "why do you call Me 'Lord, Lord' and do not do the things which I say?" His followers hear the Word, accept it, and bear fruit; they put their complete trust in Him. *Genuine faith is reflected in a true desire to love and serve God.* (Check out Luke 6:46-49 and Mark 4:20.)

The gospel—the good news that Jesus came to save sinners—is an insult to the world. Jesus said that His message of redemption would not be popular, but that it would be an offense to the world. He spoke the truth because of His love for the lost. We should seek to do the same. I believe that people respect the truth and are hungry for it. *We are to do what is right, not what is popular.*

Good is never good enough. We are declared right before God when we put our trust in Christ, not in our "good" works. This is often referred to as "justification by grace through faith alone." In passages where Jesus referred to helping those in need, following Him unconditionally, and dying to self, *He was not saying that we are saved because we do these things, but rather, we do these things because we are*

> We don't accept Christ anymore than a man drowning accepts a life preserver; we reach out and hold on for dear life.

saved. "My good works grow out of God's working within me" (J.I. Packer).

The cross, sin, and repentance have never been popular terms even though they are at the heart of the Christian faith. As a result, many today water down, or avoid altogether, these foundational truths; thus giving people a false sense of security. They want the Bible to be more appealing and marketable. *This often leaves people confused and deceived because they believe in a cross-less Christianity that bears no resemblance to Jesus's sobering call to repentance.* For this reason, it's been said that one of the greatest mission fields in the world today is the church, as a whole, in America.

If current statistics hold true, many young adults will continue to reject Christ, never to return; or, they will embrace a glamorized Christianity and be led astray. Life is a battleground, not a playground! My goal, therefore, is not to be politically correct; it's to inspire you to change from the inside out. If you've never sincerely repented and trusted in Jesus Christ as your Lord and Savior, there is no better time than now. We don't accept Christ anymore than a man drowning accepts a life preserver; we reach out and hold on for dear life.

Many who are trapped in religion go through life lacking passion, direction, and purpose, often living with a sense of remorse and guilt. They wonder, "Have I been good enough?"

A relationship with Christ changes that. II Corinthians 5:17 states: "Therefore, if anyone is in Christ, he is a new creation; old things have passed away; behold, all things have become new." *Your past is forgiven, your present secure, and your future certain.* Through Christ, you are a brand new person. If you truly grasp hold of this truth, it can motivate and encourage you beyond measure. **Though the road ahead may be uncertain at times, the solid ground beneath will never shift.**

Can I lose my salvation?

A common question for many is, "Can I lose my salvation?" I've heard both sides of the argument, and only God truly knows a person's heart, but I can share a few thoughts. One thing is for certain, salvation is a gift from God that cannot be earned.

One school of thought suggests that salvation cannot be lost, as in losing your car keys, but that it can be left, as in walking away from it. This may be why Jesus spoke of the man who said in his "heart": *my master delays His coming; therefore, I will turn from living a godly life.* When the master returned unexpectedly, the servant was banished because he chose to turn from what he knew to be right. In another passage, Jesus said, "You have left your first love," when speaking to the church in Ephesus (Revelation 2:4). James 5:19-20 adds, *if anyone wanders from the truth and someone turns him back, a soul is saved from death.* If anything, these Scriptures, and many more, reinforce the fact that we have certain responsibilities. We should never turn from what we know to be right. Jesus encouraged His followers to be watchful, prepared, and ready for His return. Are we watchful? Are we prepared? Are we ready? You don't want to live your life with a question mark here. (Read Matthew 24:45-51; Luke 21:34.)

The other school of thought suggests that some of those passages are dealing with people who never fully surrendered to Christ. As a result, they fell away. They heard the gospel, but never fully embraced it and turned from their sins; they only had "intellectual" knowledge of salvation. According to this view, the real question isn't, "Can a person lose their salvation?" but, "Was the person really saved to begin with?" Titus 1:16 and James 2:14 both conclude that many people "say" that they know God, but deny Him by their lifestyle. I John 2:19 suggests that those who acknowledge Christ initially, but deny Him later, are not saved to begin with: "They went out from us, but they were not of us; for if they had been of us, they would have continued with us."

We all sin and fall short, but the important question to ask is what is the condition of your heart—have you truly repented and believed in Christ as your Lord and Savior, or are you trusting in religion and tradition? This may be why Paul said in II Corinthians 13:5, "Examine yourself as

" When people find that after being in the church for years they are not making much progress, they ought to examine themselves and wonder whether they have been truly converted. "

—A.W. TOZER

to whether you are in the faith. Test yourselves. Do you not know yourselves, that Jesus Christ is in you?" Again, our actions do reveal a great deal about our relationship with Christ. A.W. Tozer said: "When people find that after being in the church for years they are not making much progress, they ought to examine themselves and wonder whether they have been truly converted."⁹ He added: "True conversion means radical repentance, a changed life, conscious forgiveness of sin, and a spiritual rebirth." Hebrews 3:13 warns us not to "be hardened through the deceitfulness of sin." Has your heart become so hard as to reject Jesus Christ? If so, you can change that today. I'm aware that I'm driving this point home, but I'd rather err on the side of speaking too much about a committed relationship with Jesus than too little.

As a word of encouragement to those who are struggling, consider this comparison that I heard. A pig and a lamb both find their way to the mud. The mud represents the sin that we all fall into from time to time. The pig wallows in and enjoys the mud, and may even lead others in; the lamb hates its condition and cries out. That's the difference: do you continually return and enjoy wallowing in sin, or do you regret and hate your condition when you slip in? The person who has made sin a lifestyle enjoys the sin; a follower of Christ regrets it, does what he or she can to avoid it, and cries out for forgiveness when stuck. *It's not about perfection but direction.*

Although we've discussed personal choices and things we can do, we cannot forget the fact that we don't choose God as if He's sitting in heaven waiting to be chosen. He chooses us. He invites us. He calls us. In John 6:44 Jesus said, "No one can come to Me unless the Father who sent Me draws him."

Charles Spurgeon said, "Men do not seek God first; God seeks them first; and if any of you are seeking him today it is because he has first sought you."[10] The relationship between God's sovereignty and man's responsibility is interwoven throughout the Scriptures. Our responsibility is to repent and to believe, and to live a life that reflects that decision. "God's law will not save me, but it can instruct, warn, and guide me" (J.I. Packer).

Granted, life will seem unclear and confusing at times, but God promises that He will guide you. Had I become angry and unwilling to change my rebellious attitude toward God, only the Lord knows where I'd be today. Don't let discouragement and failure stand in your way. I could write an entire book on my failures, but instead, I strive to follow the apostle Paul's advice and I encourage you to do the same: *forget about those things that are behind you. Instead reach forward to those things that are ahead of you* (Philippians 3:13). Forget your past mistakes, but remember the lessons learned because of them.

❝ I believe in Christianity as I believe that the sun has risen: not only because I see it, but because by it I see everything else. ❞

—C.S. LEWIS

As you move forward and draw from God's wisdom for guidance, you will understand why C.S. Lewis said, "I believe in Christianity as I believe that the sun has risen: not only because I see it, but because by it I see everything else."[11]

The greatest need today— unlocking spiritual power

If you find yourself confused or worried about your relationship with Christ, let me reassure you: if you've acknowledged that you are in need of a Savior and have genuinely repented of your sins, and, through faith, have accepted the fact that Jesus died for you, your uncertainty may be coming from "spiritual malnutrition"—you need more spiritual food!

For many years, when a book or resource was recommended to me, especially the Bible, I said, "No thanks, I'm not a reader. Plus, I'm too busy." But when I truly trusted in Jesus Christ and prayed for a strong desire to serve Him, and sought God with all of my heart, something changed. I studied the Bible daily, listened to countless hours of sermons, and read dozens of Christian books and biographies. I couldn't get enough. Granted, not everyone will experience the same type of intensity—God prepares us for different ministries; however, hunger for knowledge of Him should be real and evident.

Looking back, I avoided reading the Bible because my spiritual life was unhealthy. In the medical field, hunger is often a sign of health. When we're sick, we're often not hungry. In the same way, our spiritual hunger is often related to our spiritual health. **God's Word is to our spirit what food is to our body.** If there is a lack of hunger for God's Word and spiritual growth, the spirit is weak and unhealthy. Jesus said that *man does not live on bread alone, but by every word that comes from the mouth of God* (Matthew 4:4). We need spiritual food.

Generally, we wouldn't think of going without food. Why then do we often neglect God-given spiritual food that is far

❝ *What can a hammer do without the hand that grasps it, and what can we do without the Spirit of God?* **❞**

—CHARLES SPURGEON

more necessary? And why aren't more people serving Christ passionately? One reason is because we often overlook the work of God's Spirit in our lives. One of the wonderful things about having a relationship with Jesus is that the Holy Spirit resides in us.

The Holy Spirit is not some weird, mystical force; He's part of the triune nature of God. The Bible says that the Spirit intercedes, leads, guides, teaches, and so on. (Check out Romans 8:26; Acts 8:29; John 16:13.) He enables and empowers us to hunger and thirst for righteousness, and to boldly live for Christ. God's Word becomes living and active in the life of the believer who is continually *filled* with the Holy Spirit (Ephesians 5:18). Charles Spurgeon said it best, "What can a hammer do without the hand that grasps it, and what can we do without the Spirit of God?"[12]

If you doubt the role of the Holy Spirit in the life of a Christian, simply read the New Testament Book of *Acts*. If God seems distant, Bible study boring, and church irrelevant, it's probably because the work of the Holy Spirit is being suppressed. More change will be seen outwardly as the Holy Spirit is given more power to rule inwardly.

It's possible to be "Bible taught," but not "Spirit led," thus making spiritual issues boring and dry. **The Scriptures, to be understood, must be read with the same Spirit**

that originally inspired them. Understanding God's Word and living a victorious Christian life can only be achieved by the power of the Holy Spirit. If the Holy Spirit inspired the Scriptures, and Jesus and the Apostles began their ministry in the power of the Spirit, we would be wise to ask for His guidance as well.

I sincerely believe that the greatest need in the lives of Christians today is the power of the Holy Spirit. It's been said that if the power of the Holy Spirit were removed from the early church, 90 percent of the work would have ceased. Unfortunately, it appears that if the Holy Spirit were removed from the church today, 90 percent of the work would continue. Sadly, the only thing holding many churches together today is social activity, not the activity of the Spirit. It's been said that if Christianity today (as a whole) were a poison, it would harm no one, and if it were a medicine, it would cure no one. As incredible as this sounds, it may be true, at least to some degree—**when we fail to embrace the Spirit's power, we become powerless**.

Are you willing to be completely obedient to the Spirit and surrender your life to Him? *Many are not willing to give up all to gain all.* The desire to be filled must be a priority. Granted, there is a difference between receiving the Holy Spirit when we place our trust in Christ, and the filling that occurs as we fervently seek the Lord. Every area of our life should be affected as we surrender to His influence. This is why some people are more sensitive to the things of God; they are filled with the Holy Spirit.

In the book mentioned earlier about the life of Billy Graham, the author wrote of another time early in Billy's ministry when a Welsh evangelist told Mr. Graham how God

> **"** *... a true work of the Holy Spirit would be evident: it would elevate the truth, exalt Christ, oppose Satan, point people to the Scriptures, and result in love for God and others.* **"**
>
> **—JONATHAN EDWARDS**

completely turned his life around by the power of the Holy Spirit. Billy desired this same power and prayed for it. The story concludes that Billy Graham was a new man from that day forward and that the world was going to hear from him; he was, and it did.[13] This is also true in the lives of many great men and women who were, and are, bold witnesses for Christ. Boldness comes directly from the Holy Spirit. No wonder the enemy wants to discredit and disregard the work of the Holy Spirit. "If the Lord's people were only half as eager to be filled with the Spirit as they are to prove that they cannot be filled, the church would be crowded out" (Tozer).

The power of the Holy Spirit is like dynamite that ignites a hunger for God so intense that every aspect of life is changed—we become bold, not passive; stable, not fanatical; and committed, not wavering. In the early years of American history, during the First Great Awakening, Pastor Jonathan Edwards said that a true work of the Holy Spirit would be evident: it would elevate the truth, exalt Christ, oppose Satan, point people to the Scriptures, and result in love for God and others.

Unfortunately, many confuse a Spirit-filled life with sheer emotionalism. Emotions aren't necessarily a reflection of a changed heart, but a changed heart should be reflected in our emotions. When truth penetrates the heart, excitement and enthusiasm often follow; these emotions can be good and God-given. I'm not suggesting that extreme fanaticism and weird behavior are marks of someone filled with the Spirit—as D. Martyn Lloyd-Jones said: *never interpret Scripture in the light of your experiences, but rather, interpret your experiences in the penetrating light of Scripture.*

As Christians, we are given the Holy Spirit, but what we do with Him is largely up to us—we can quench and grieve Him, thus causing Him to withdraw, or we can truly surrender our life to His influence. (Read I Thessalonians 5:19 and Ephesians 4:30.) Often, the only thing standing between the work of the Holy Spirit and us is our will. The Holy Spirit will not empower you to do what you want to do; He will only empower you to do what God wants you to do. Pray for the Spirit's influence, desire it above all else, and continually live a life that glorifies Christ—*the Holy Spirit is given to those who obey God* (Acts 5:32).

Spiritual maturity is not a prerequisite for the filling of the Spirit. You can be filled when you submit your life to His power. **"We are leaky vessels, and have to be kept right under the fountain all the time in order to keep full"** (D.L. Moody). Stay under the fountain.

Without a shadow of doubt, the difference between "saying" that we are Christians and actually living a life empowered by the Holy Spirit, is as different as night and day. The Christian life can be exciting and full of passion when the Holy Spirit reigns in the believer, but boring and dull when He does not. The reason why so many lack peace, joy, and contentment is often because they are not listening to the inner promptings of the Holy Spirit. These promptings confront wrong attitudes, destructive habits, and certain tendencies that damper our spiritual life. The Scriptures make it clear that God's power will not flow until sin is dealt with—obedience empowers!

When I think of the power of the Holy Spirit, I sometimes think of the time when I worked as a heavy equipment operator. On one particular day, I forgot the key. There I sat behind the wheel with all this potential power, but this enormous machine was powerless without the key. In the same way, the Holy Spirit is the key that unlocks and releases spiritual power within our lives. As a matter of fact, many go from relationship to relationship, drug to drug, or religion to religion searching for someone or something to fill a need. As a result, their lives are often filled with depression, anxiety, and fear simply because they fail to embrace the work of the Holy Spirit. I wish that more time could be spent on this topic because I sincerely believe that the power of the Holy Spirit is a wonderful gift from God, don't take it for granted. God wants you to be filled with the Holy Spirit.

Questions to consider for Chapter Two:

1. Why do people want to outlaw or slander Jesus's name, remove His words from the public sector, and tarnish His reputation? Why are those who claim to be "tolerant" often intolerant of Christianity? Is it because Jesus said that *He is the only way, the only truth, and the only life* (John 14:6)?

2. Do you agree that religion is often associated with following rules? Are you trying to follow rules instead of allowing a relationship to guide you?

3. How can we keep watchful care of God's commandments? Remember, loving the Lord with all your heart, soul, and mind is the greatest commandment.

4. Do you agree that the only thing standing between the work of the Holy Spirit and you is your will? How do you feel about this statement: the Holy Spirit will not empower you to do what you want to do, but He will empower you to do what God wants you to do.

5. Do you truly have a personal relationship with Jesus Christ? If you are not sure, now is the time to commit your life. We are not guaranteed tomorrow!

Recommended Reading:
Why Grace Changes Everything by Chuck Smith
Hard to Believe by John MacArthur
The Best of A.W. Tozer compiled by Warren W. Wiersbe
The Holy Spirit by Billy Graham
Living Water by Chuck Smith

God doesn't call the qualified—
He qualifies the called.

———————

A "good" thing isn't always
a "God" thing.

CHAPTER THREE

WHAT IS
God's Will
for My Life?

Your greatest investment

"I*T'S ALMOST TOO LATE*" jumped from the pages as I read an article by noted author and speaker, Josh McDowell. He stated that the reason so many young people are losing ground in the area of spiritual truth is because their parents are not involved in teaching them in word or action. He continued, "One of the most common questions I get is, 'How could we live for Christ, when we don't want the Christ that our parents have?' "[14] Wow, that should force us all to ask, "Who am I influencing, and who's influencing me?" Now, more than ever, it's time to make solid choices in unstable times. *When the deterioration of the family is coming from within the same walls that were designed to protect it, it's time for change.*

"What does this have to do with God's will?" you may ask. A great deal. If you are a parent, or plan to be one, your greatest investment will be in your children—period! Your goal may be to own a business, climb the corporate ladder, or pursue a profession; whatever you choose, there is no greater opportunity than to promote the spiritual success of another, especially your child's. Proverbs 22:6 (NIV) reminds us, "Train a child in the way he should go, and when he is old he will not turn from it." **Character is not only taught; it's caught.** It's demonstrated through the lives of parents.

We live in a society that emphasizes wealth and possessions, but these things have no eternal value. I hardly remember my parents' income or many of the material things they gave me. I do, however, remember the values they taught, those things that money cannot buy. It's been well stated that the best things in life aren't things. Although I took a temporary detour in my younger years, my parents' example left a lasting impression. Never underestimate the power of parenting!

It's possible to succeed in business, but fail at home. Look around, it's happening everywhere, from the pulpit to the boardroom. Unfortunately, the price of success is often paid at the family's expense. A friend of mine once shared a tragic story. He told of a trip to the hospital to visit a man who was dying. The man could no longer speak; he could, however, write. What followed was more devastating. The man cried as he wrote. At the top of his list he wrote that he regretted not spending more time with his family. He was in anguish over the fact that he had not been a better father and husband, but, instead, had built his life around other things. When all is said and done, it's devastating to find that

... the more that I owned, the more that owned me. Money can be a great servant, but a terrible master.

life was invested in those things that hold no lasting value. Be grateful and consider it a privilege that God has given you the ability to make a difference in the life of another.

I just want to be 'happy'

If you believe that wealth makes people happy, think again. Money can buy the best mattress, but it can't buy sleep. Why do millionaires, movie stars, and top entertainers often turn to spirituality, drugs, and alcohol if success satisfies? They discover that money and fame are not the answers. Celebrities frequently admit being happy when their career produces fame and fortune but very unhappy when it doesn't. Many of us do the same thing: we often measure happiness by what's "happening" to us. **When things go right, we're happy; when things go wrong, we're unhappy. If happiness is always measured by our circumstances, the road ahead is going to be very disappointing.**

One of the best times in my life was when I went from working seventy hours a week as a corporate executive running multiple fitness locations to making much less money working in construction and writing books. During that transition I realized that *the more that I owned, the more that owned me.* Money can be a great servant, but a terrible master.

❝❝Those that follow Christ must not expect great or high things in this world. **❞❞**

—MATTHEW HENRY

Even though God cares about the smallest details of our lives, His will focuses primarily on spiritual growth, not on material things. We, however, often focus on physical things: a nice car, a huge bank account, and a large home. But even with all this, we can still lack fulfillment. We want what we *think* will make us happy—God wants to develop our character and conform us into the image of His Son. (See Romans 8:29.) Although the desire for marriage, college, career, and finances are important, they should not be our primary focus.

The 'true' measure of success

Proverbs 13:12 states, "Hope deferred makes the heart sick, but when the desire comes, it is a tree of life." When our godly desires are being fulfilled, joy is brought to our lives. The goal, then, is to align our desires with God's. God wants us to experience a fulfilled and abundant life. An abundant life can include material wealth, but it does not depend on it, nor does it focus on it. "Those that follow Christ must not expect great or high things in this world" (Matthew Henry).[15] Problems arise when we seek money, status, and recognition instead of the things of God—when we pursue prosperity instead of our God-given passion. Literally millions of people are unhappy today because they chose a lucrative career rather than a career that they were gifted for and would enjoy. **Many are living, but there's no life in their years.**

As you move into dating, and eventually marriage, this truth becomes a reality. For instance, a husband may want a large home, expensive cars, and lots of money, but that's not what his wife and children will need. They'll first need to feel a sense of spiritual leadership, security, and understanding. Proverbs 23:4 (NIV) says, "Do not wear yourself out to get rich; have the wisdom to show restraint." When we wear ourselves out in the pursuit of wealth, relationships suffer— period. This is not God's will.

When I worked in the corporate world, my workweek was spent crunching numbers, reviewing revenue lines, hitting board-allocated budgets, and auditing departments. Ultimately, I gave up so much for so little. I was not afforded the luxury of being involved in the lives of others to the degree that I am now. Those who are the most fulfilled are often those who focus on making a difference in the lives of others. My advice: **focus on the blessings that you do have, not on the things that you don't have.** Your career should follow, not precede, a relationship with God and your family. *If you want to truly know what's important to you, simply review how you spend your time and your money.* It's difficult to be in the center of God's will when priorities are misaligned.

Proverbs 1:19 (NLT) says, "Such is the fate of all who are greedy for gain. It ends up robbing them of life." I want to stress this point, especially to men. To be robbed of life often means to be robbed of joy, peace, and contentment. **Ironically, self-centeredness takes from your life, rather than gives.** Although difficult, focus on making a positive difference in the lives of others. You'll never regret that decision.

God has called all of us to minister to one another. Some may have the calling of a professional, a technician, a pastor, a contractor, and/or one of the highest callings of all, a parent; yet, they still lack fulfillment, largely because of their definition of success.

For example, a singer may cut demo tapes and promote their music year after year, but their career never takes off. They see other artists succeeding and wonder why they are not. Maybe the question shouldn't be, "Why am I not succeeding?" but rather, "Am I pursuing my God-given purpose?" In other words, how are we measuring success? Maybe we should redefine our definition of success. Is there a difference between a musician who sells millions of CDs worldwide compared to the person who sings at church, touches dozens of lives, and attends to the daily needs of his or her family? Society may believe that there is a huge difference—one is a "success," the other is not, but God looks at the heart rather than the outward appearance (I Samuel 16:7). It may be that both are successful in His eyes. Surely He blesses some people with prosperity and recognition, but, in many cases, the one who appears least is actually greater. As Oswald Chambers states: "God buries His men [and women] in the midst of paltry things, no monuments are erected to them; they are ignored, not because they are unworthy, but because they are in the place where they cannot be seen."[16]

Be careful how you measure success. Are you trying to be the best, or trying to do your best? Doing your best, and being the best spring from different motives. When we try to "be the best," we may have the tendency to compete and compromise our character, thus lowering our standards in the pursuit of being No. 1. Strive for excellence and make every effort to accomplish your goals, but test your motives. (Check out Colossians 3:23.)

Using your gifts to help others, especially those who cannot offer anything in return, is God's will; it leads to fulfillment. Is it always easy? Not at all, but when we reflect on how blessed we are as a nation and how gracious God has been, we can be encouraged and motivated to help others. This is the "true" measure of success.

Keys to pursuing God's will

Let me begin by applauding your desire to know God's will; this is a sign of spiritual health. God guides those who are willing to follow.

When it comes to knowing God's will, more often than not, unless it's written in His Word, there are no specific answers. For instance, the Bible doesn't say who to marry or where to work, but it does offer important principles that lead you in the right direction. However, there are some things that are clearly God's will for our lives: *to be saved and to worship Him, to be holy and set apart for His glory, to be filled continually with the Holy Spirit, to witness to others, to make disciples,* and so on. (Refer to I Timothy 2:4; I Thessalonians 4:3-7; Ephesians 5:17-18; and Matthew 28:19.)

Although the following pages will not outline God's specific will for your life, they will provide guidance for the journey.

> **Make a relationship with Christ your top priority.** Throughout my teen years, my father often took us trap shooting. As soon as the clay target was released into the air, we'd raise our shotguns and fire. There were only seconds to aim and fire as the round target darted through the air. If we lost sight of the target, we would miss the shot; the same holds true with

knowing God's will. If we neglect to focus on the target, which is our personal relationship with Jesus Christ, we can miss God's most productive plan for our life. This is the most important aspect of knowing God's will. Start here.

> **Realize that a "good" thing isn't necessarily a God thing.** "So teach us to number our days, that we may gain a heart of wisdom" (Psalm 90:12). When we number our days, we're more inclined to use them wisely. Taking on too many responsibilities and commitments often leads to frustration and failure. Realize that you'll have to say "no" to some things and stay committed to others. There are also seasons in life—at times you'll be able to do more, at other times, less. *Moderation and commitment are spiritual principles that play an important role in pursuing God's will.*

For instance, after my first few books were published, I was invited to speak on several occasions. I was also asked to teach at study groups and speak at church conferences. In addition, I was writing other books, reading unending material, studying the Bible regularly, spending time with my family, helping out at church, overseeing two websites, and working in construction. I was glad to help when I could, but my time was extremely limited. I had to decline many "good" things.

There were times when I could have done more, and there were times when I should have done less. It was at that time that I realized how important it was to focus primarily on the path that God has chosen for me, because a "good" thing isn't always a "God" thing. We should never allow our relationship with Christ to suffer because we're too busy. The things that we do "for" God

The things that we do "for" God should not replace our time "with" God. Jesus took time to pray and seek God's will; He was very effective but never "too busy."

should not replace our time "with" God. Jesus took time to pray and seek God's will; He was very effective but never "too busy." We're often too busy because we're doing too much. *Sometimes it's better to do a few things really well than many things halfheartedly.* This doesn't mean that we should decline opportunities to serve in order to spend more time watching television or playing video games; it means that we should be selective when committing to certain things. Once we commit to something, it's important that we see it through. (This also applies to returning phone calls and emails, and to helping others.) Avoid getting involved in long-term commitments only to quit a few weeks later, unless there are unforeseen circumstances. It honors God when you keep your word.

> **Pursue the desire that God has placed in "your" heart.** "Commit your works to the LORD, and your thoughts will be established" (Proverbs 16:3). You may have a desire to pursue a medical degree, or to help the homeless in your area, while your friend may have a passion to become an attorney, and yet another friend may want to pursue politics. Problems

God doesn't call the qualified—
He qualifies the called. A degree
from the Master is far more
valuable than a masters degree.

occur when we compete with one another, or when we try to force our views and opinions on others, and vice versa. Case in point: although some people encouraged me to start a fitness business similar to the one that I left, I knew that God had other plans, and I pursued those plans regardless of what others suggested. This doesn't mean that we shouldn't seek counsel, because we should; godly advice is very important, but when it comes to pursuing God-given dreams, others may not share your vision. A.W. Tozer did not attend a seminary or a university, or even a Bible school, even though many people encouraged him to do so; yet, he left writings and books that have inspired and motivated countless people throughout the years. Remember: God doesn't call the qualified—He qualifies the called. A degree from the Master is far more valuable than a masters degree. With all that said, education should be a proper priority in your life. The key is to put your trust in God, not in education, and to pursue the desire that He has placed in "your" heart.

> *Frequently check your reasons for pursuing your goals.* "Let nothing be done through selfish ambition or conceit, but in lowliness of mind let each esteem others better than himself" (Philippians 2:3). If

you're pursuing dreams solely to impress others, or for financial gain, you're on the wrong path. **God clearly blesses and provides, but our motives must stem from a pure heart.** But how do we evaluate motives? Here are just a few helpful questions: would you go on a mission trip, visit the elderly, donate money, or help the homeless even if no one knew? Would you sing on the praise and worship team if you had to sing from the back and not from center stage? Would you be in leadership if you were not recognized and applauded for your efforts? Answers to these types of questions reveal a great deal about personal motives. *Serving must come from a true desire to help, not from self-glorification.* Difficult as it may seem, it can be done if we frequently check our reasons for pursuing goals, dreams, and aspirations.

The inner promptings of the Holy Spirit are like gauges in an airplane—if the pilot ignores them, he'll miss his destination.

> **Regularly ask, "Is God truly guiding me?"**
"I will instruct you and teach you in the way you should go; I will guide you with My eye" (Psalm 32:8). The inner promptings of the Holy Spirit are like gauges in an airplane—if the pilot ignores them, he'll miss his destination. The conviction of the Holy Spirit is a wonderful gift from God—listen to it.

I often hear people say, "God is leading me to do this or that," and all too often, they find that they made a very poor decision. What happened? The Holy Spirit didn't lead them; human nature and emotions did. Many jump into a dating relationship or marriage, buy an expensive vehicle or recreational toy, or charge thousands of dollars on credit, believing that God's Spirit is leading them. I'm amazed at the number of people who don't help those in need, budget their income, or make smart financial decisions, and still think that they are using wisdom in the area of finances. I'm equally alarmed at the number of couples who are convinced that God is leading them toward marriage, yet they engage in pre-marital sex and are considering living together before marriage. Let me be clear: God directs us to make "wise" decisions that correspond with His word. *Disobedience leads to disappointment.* That's why it's always sensible to ask, "Is God truly guiding me?" before making an important decision. **Furthermore, if you're not in the Word, the Word won't be in you.** One of the best ways to know if God is truly guiding you is to stay and obey—stay in His Word; obey His principles. "God is more likely to direct me through wise teaching than through inner voices" (J.I. Packer).

> *Step out and serve.* "Whoever desires to become great among you, let him be your servant" (Matthew 20:26). Although difficult at times, I've found that it's simply best to start serving. Whether it's helping families in need, donating your time to special events, hosting a Bible study, ushering at church, helping clean up after events, or serving in the community—**God directs as we serve.** Often, a person may not know their calling or God's will for their life until they step out and serve. "The humble He teaches His way" (Psalm 25:9).

❝❝ *Integrity is one of several paths. It distinguishes itself from the others because it is the right path, and the only one upon which you will never get lost.* ❞❞

—M.H. McKEE

> ***Allow integrity to guide you.*** "A life of moral excellence leads to knowing God better" (II Peter 1:5 NLT). One of the best ways to know God's will is to live morally upright by letting honesty and integrity guide your decisions. M.H. McKee states it well, "Integrity is one of several paths. It distinguishes itself from the others because it is the right path, and the only one upon which you will never get lost." Proverbs 11:3 adds, "The integrity of the upright will guide them." Combine integrity, wisdom, counsel, and prayer, and you'll have a better grasp on who to marry, where to work, what school to attend, and so on. Unfortunately, we want to hear from God first and work on character later, but God desires that we work on character first, and then we'll be better able to hear. Of course a new believer in Christ can sense God's will in many areas, but, in general, maturity brings clarity. That's why "a life of moral excellence leads to knowing God better."

> ***Learn to sense God's direction through the guidance of the Holy Spirit.*** "When He, the Spirit of truth, has come, He will guide you into all truth" (John 16:13). Should I date? Should I attend

college or begin a career? Should I do this or that? The "Should I's" can be endless, and it can become frustrating at times. God told Abraham in Genesis 12:1, *go to a land that I will show you.* Abraham didn't know "exactly" where to go, but he trusted God to direct him. In the same way, God teaches us to sense His direction through faith and the guidance of the Holy Spirit, but be careful: **there's a very fine line between presumption and faith.** That's why it's critical that we spend time each day reading God's Word and praying for direction. We can't presume that we know what direction to take— we must ask, and, often, wait. If we don't ask, He may not answer. Sometimes we do experience a true sense of God's exact direction, but often, we simply walk by faith. Concerning major decisions such as marriage, college, and career choices, it's best to move forward at an even slower pace. Proverbs 3:6 reminds us to *commit "all" our ways to God and trust that He will direct us and make our path smooth.*

> **Compare your "feelings" to the Word.** "The heart is deceitful above all things, and desperately wicked; who can know it?" (Jeremiah 17:9). **Feelings shouldn't lead but follow.** Although feelings can be good and God-ordained (I thank God for the love that I feel toward God and my family), when it comes to making decisions, we shouldn't interpret the Scriptures in the light of our feelings, but rather, interpret our feelings through the light of Scripture. For instance, how often have you sensed a leading and are not sure if it's God or not, especially when dating? A good question to ask is, "Am I allowing my feelings to control my choices?" Attraction is important, but if attraction is

Attraction is important, but if attraction is the only thing that holds a couple together, marriage is going to be a very difficult journey.

the only thing that holds a couple together, márriage is going to be a very difficult journey. Countless couples say that they are in love, when, in reality, they are attracted—their feelings are in control. Being drawn by physical attraction, depending on the situation, is not wrong; God-given chemistry is important. Although I was greatly attracted to my wife's physical beauty, it was her inner qualities that held me. Both chemistry and character are essential; it's important to value the person beneath the beauty.

As you move forward in a dating or courting relationship, frequently evaluate your reasons for pursuing the relationship. Are you intrigued with beauty or good looks so much so that serious character flaws are overlooked? If so, rethink the relationship and ask, "Am I dating, or going to marry this person simply because they are attractive? Are my feelings controlling me?"

Remember, God's will always corresponds with His Word. Contrary to God's Word, many Christians date and marry unbelievers. "It just 'feels' right," they say. Regardless of feelings, God's Word does not change. Sharing the same beliefs (being equally yoked) is not just a good idea, it's God's principle intended to promote the "long-term" success of a relationship. The more we ignore God's principles and the conviction of the Holy Spirit, the harder it becomes to hear His voice; we become spiritually deaf. For example, if you are dating and sense that you are in a wrong relationship, step away and take time to analyze your feelings. I often wonder how many people make poor choices simply because they are in a hurry. You can rarely go wrong by waiting for direction, but you can often go wrong by rushing. The transition from being single, to dating, to marriage should be a slow progression for most. **Don't abort a potential blessing simply because you're in a hurry—feelings come and go.**

Use every situation for God's glory. If you are single, use that opportunity to build and strengthen your character, and care for the things of God. If you are dating, use that time to seek God more fervently, and pray for guidance and direction. If you are healing from a past relationship, learn from the experience. Be assured that all things can work together for good as we commit our lives to Him.

As another example, if you are considering such things as getting a tattoo or having your body pierced, don't rush the decision. Take time and ponder the long-term consequences. Let's be clear: God has given us

If a comfort which you think you need, and which appears to you to be very sweet, does not glorify Christ, look very suspiciously upon it.

—CHARLES SPURGEON

the freedom to choose. Tattoos, piercings, or other fads are not going to make the difference in your salvation, but they may be decisions that you'll later regret. And remember, just because something "feels" or "looks" good doesn't mean that it is. Although we might state this differently today, Charles Spurgeon said, "If a comfort which you think you need, and which appears to you to be very sweet, does not glorify Christ, look very suspiciously upon it."17

> **Use wisdom and move in the right direction.**
"Wisdom is the principal thing; therefore get wisdom ... when you walk, your steps will not be hindered" (Proverbs 4:7; 4:12). Although this principle may have been stated previously, it bears repeating. One time when I clearly did not use wisdom happened when I owned a vehicle with very low mileage, and it was paid for. Instead of keeping it and avoiding monthly payments for years to come, I went against God's leading and traded it for a new vehicle with high payments; it just **felt** right. That unwise decision followed me for years.

When we know what to do through the promptings of the Holy Spirit and godly counsel, and through the confirmation of Scripture, we need to respond with wisdom. In your case, using wisdom could easily mean continuing down the same path that you're on, ending a bad relationship, or forgiving someone who has wronged you. God can use you at school, on the job, and at home. *The Lord simply asks that we live right; that we focus on being a merciful and forgiving person, and that we walk humbly with Him* (Micah 6:8). **"God may not tell me what he is planning, but he lets me know how he wants me to live"** (J.I. Packer).

> *Patiently and quietly listen.* You'll have to engage the fruit of the Spirit here, especially self-control. "It is better to be patient than powerful; it is better to have self-control than to conquer a city" (Proverbs 16:32 NLT). Patient people deliberately take their time and examine the possibilities, weigh the consequences, seek guidance, and do what they believe to be right. Self-control allows us to control our desires and emotions rather than allowing them to control us. **I rarely hear, "I moved too slowly," but I often hear, "I moved too quickly."** Slow down! It's worth the wait.

I've found that God doesn't always answer "yes" or "no" to questions that don't require an immediate response. He tells us to wait. It's in this waiting period that we develop patience and trust. His leading isn't a reckless course of action; it's a well-designed plan that often takes time to unfold. However, it's incredibly difficult to hear from God if we're actively engaging in sin. Sin means *to miss the mark.* We can't be on target in the center of God's will if we're continually missing the mark. It's like trying to hit a bull's-eye with a bent arrow. It doesn't matter how attractive the sin is, or how good it makes you feel, remove it from your life. Remember, biblical principles do not change with the times.

Are you anxious to hear from God? If so, set aside time each day solely for prayer, journaling, and the reading of His Word. Throughout the Bible, God often spoke to people during times of isolation. He spoke to Moses on the backside of the desert, and to the prophet Elijah in a cave. He communicated to the apostle Paul while Paul was in prison, and to the apostle John while he was in exile. Throughout history, those who have

God's voice leads, not pushes; stills, not rushes; calms, not obsesses; reassures, not frightens.

followed God have spent time in prayer and Scripture study. "We must spend much time on our knees before God if we are to continue in the power of the Holy Spirit" (R.A. Torrey).

Why does God want us to set aside time for this? For one, it won't happen on its own. Second, a busy life leaves little room for communicating with God. He's asking, "How bad do you want a relationship with Me?" Like it or not, actions still speak louder than words. In order to hear the still, small voice of the Holy Spirit, it's necessary to leave the activity of the day and deliberately listen. God's voice leads, not pushes; stills, not rushes; calms, not obsesses; reassures, not frightens.

When God spoke to Elijah in I Kings 19:11-12, the Scriptures state that *a fierce wind blew, the earth quaked, and fire came, but God was not in them. He was, however, in the still, small voice that followed.* God wants our undivided attention each and every day. This will mean turning off the television, the Internet, or the video game, but again, how bad do you want to know God's will? It's never too late to start, or to renew your relationship with Him.

> ***Keep moving; don't become idle.*** "In all labor there is profit, but idle chatter leads only to poverty"

(Proverbs 14:23). Labor is another word for effort; idle is another word for inactivity. Effort produces results; inactivity doesn't! Those things in life worth having generally take energy to achieve. You might ask, "If we are to patiently wait and quietly listen, how can we keep moving?" *Although there are clearly times when God wants us to wait, it's difficult to direct what's not moving.* I mentioned earlier that during my childhood and teen years, my family often vacationed in the Eastern Sierra Nevada Mountain Range near June Lake, California. On one occasion (when I was very young), we stopped on the lake to fish. After the motor was turned off, I tried steering the boat. No matter which direction I turned the wheel, the boat stood still. I asked my dad why the boat wasn't working. He said that it was working, but that I could not steer something that was not moving. In the same way, God may be directing us, but we'll get nowhere if we're not moving. For example, if you're not sure which college to attend or career to pursue, pray about it, seek godly counsel, weigh the options, submit applications, use wisdom, consider your motives, and move forward. Moving forward doesn't mean heading out without an agenda or a plan; it means exploring your options, serving God and others, and doing your best each and every day. Keep moving.

> **God's will is often revealed over time.**
"With the Lord one day is as a thousand years, and a thousand years as one day" (II Peter 3:8). Although this Scripture may not apply directly to God's will in the context of our discussion, the principle still applies: His will is revealed in His time. Granted, there are times when the Holy Spirit directs us instantly—prompting a

phone call to a friend in need, or leading us to make a quick decision, but when it comes to the big picture, we sometimes only see portions of it. God often leads us through one open door at a time. **"When God calls me, he makes it possible for me to move in the direction he is leading"** (J.I. Packer). For example, when I felt an inner conviction to leave an eight-year profession, I only saw glimpses of the big picture. Although it seemed very unlikely at the time, I saw myself writing books and speaking. I had no idea how it would all unfold, but I knew that I needed to have faith and trust God no matter how long it took. God began to open doors, and I walked through. Additionally, I had peace. In the same way, you may not know exactly what you are going to do with your life, but God does. Be patient.

God may lead more by withholding information than by supplying it. This can help us stay focused on the task at hand, remain obedient, and walk by faith. For example, had I known that I was going to encounter a few years of financial hardship and dig ditches for a living when I stepped away from a six-figure income, I might not have left. I only saw glimpses of His will for a reason: He wanted me to pay attention to where I was as well as where I was going. Enjoy each and every day, and don't be in a hurry.

> ***Don't be surprised by challenges.*** "We are hard-pressed on every side, yet not crushed; we are perplexed, but not in despair" (II Corinthians 4:8). When we are walking according to God's will, the struggles that we encounter are *not* necessarily an indicator that we are out of God's will; He may be

molding us, or they may be part of an unfolding plan. God often directs by removing us from our comfort zone. He closes one door but opens another. God strengthens and prepares us so that we can handle the weight of what He has called us to do. Figuratively speaking, you don't see a young apple tree bear abundant fruit; the tree would collapse under the weight. We also have growing to do. There are personality issues, attitudes, and certain habits that may need to be adjusted. There is a saying in construction: *the deeper the foundation, the stronger the structure.* The depth of our spiritual foundation also determines how much we can carry. Don't be frustrated; God may be building and strengthening your foundation, and aligning your will with His.

I once believed that life was easy in the center of God's will, and if it wasn't easy then I was out of His will. This isn't necessarily true. Yes, we should have peace in the center of God's will, but not freedom from difficult circumstances. At times, we may fight bouts of anxiety, depression, and fear. Many biblical heroes fought hardship and anxiety while being in the center of God's will. How can we determine if a challenge is the result of being in God's will, or because of disobedience? First, ask yourself if your motives are pure and honest. Second, focus on obeying God's Word and the convictions of the Holy Spirit. Third, seek biblical counsel and use wisdom. He will direct you one way or the other.

Again, try to see challenges as opportunities for growth. **Being in the center of God's will does not prevent challenges; it often creates them.** In Matthew 7:24-27, Jesus tells the story of a wise man who built his house on solid rock (God's Word), rather than on shifting sand (man's philosophy). As a result, his house withstood the storm, but the foolish man who built his house on sand lost everything. Remember, both men encountered the storm. Adversity comes to all of us. Expect storms, but you can weather them successfully as you look to God's Word for the answers.

> **God's will is always what's best.** "And we know that all things work together for good to those who love God, to those who are the called according to His purpose" (Romans 8:28). As a young adult, I remember feeling that if I committed my life to God, all the fun would be over. You probably know people who feel this way—maybe that's you. Nothing could be further from the truth. Although it may not **feel** like it from time to time, God's will is always what's best. He has placed godly desires within you, and those desires will be revealed as you pursue His will. Missionaries will often say that they had a deep desire to serve God as missionaries. Many Christian businessmen and professionals also say they felt inclined toward their specific field. I, for one, could not have chosen a better path for my life. God does not give talents and interests to be wasted. He created the desires of your heart and will develop them as you seek to serve Him and others. He knows what's best.

> **His leading is often calm and reassuring.** "For God is not the author of confusion but of peace" (I Corinthians 14:33). Although there may be times of anxiety when a decision must be made, God seldom rushes us. His leading is generally calm and reassuring. Although you may feel uncertain, you should have peace before making a major decision. Peace is often a good

indicator that you are moving in the right direction, but peace alone can be deceptive. For example, when an idea comes to me, I try not to act on it immediately (note the word "try"). Depending on the circumstance, I give it a few days, maybe a few weeks, or even a few months before I pursue it. As a matter of fact, some dreams and aspirations took years to unfold, and some are still unfolding. I've learned to wait for confirmation, search the Scriptures, pray for God's leading, and see which doors open. If the desire doesn't continue, it may have simply been an emotional impulse. When you feel rushed, try to slow down, seek godly advice, and wait on God. Again, *you can rarely go wrong waiting, but you can often go wrong rushing.* If there's no time to wait, use wisdom and make the decision to the best of your ability.

> **God's will and perseverance often go hand-in-hand.** "Add to your faith virtue, to virtue knowledge, to knowledge self-control, to self-control perseverance" (II Peter 1:5-6). From time to time you may feel like giving up and returning to your familiar comfort zone. Don't! Press through. You are exercising a very important spiritual muscle called perseverance. There is a saying that ships are safest in the harbor,

You were not created to fail; you were created to succeed—make sure that you remember the true meaning of success.

but they are not made for the harbor. Remember, you were designed to weather storms successfully. When life becomes difficult and challenging, set your sight on the goal, not on the challenge. You were not created to fail; you were created to succeed—make sure that you remember the true meaning of success.

Questions to consider for Chapter Three:

1. Do you agree that there is no greater opportunity than to promote the spiritual success of another, especially if that person is your child? Why isn't this a priority for many parents? How can you be different?

2. We want what we think will make us happy—God wants to develop our character and conform us to the image of His Son. With this understanding, how can we better understand God's will?

3. If you want to truly know what's important to you, simply review how you spend your time and your money. Do your priorities need readjusting?

4. What are some ways you can begin complementing others and supporting their success rather than competing with them? Do you agree that self-centeredness takes from your life, rather than gives?

5. Briefly review the keys of *knowing God's will,* and note any areas that may require attention. What daily decisions can help you stay within God's will?

Recommended Reading:
Knowing and Doing the Will of God by J.I. Packer
The Mystery of God's Will by Chuck Swindoll
Pursuing the Will of God by Jack Hayford
How to Pray by R.A. Torrey
The Jesus Style by Gayle Erwin

Light and darkness, right and wrong, good and evil, truth and error are incompatibles … when they compromise it is the light, the right, the good, and the truth that are damaged.

—W. GRAHAM SCROGGIE

———————

What we embrace eventually embraces us.

CHAPTER FOUR

ENTERTAINMENT
Where Do I Draw the Line?

Family friend

WHEN MATT WAS VERY YOUNG, his parents introduced him to a family friend. Matt was excited because he had someone to play with; his parents were pleased because he could entertain Matt when they were busy.

As the years went by, Matt and his friend spent countless hours together playing video games, watching sports, music videos, and reality shows. In time, things changed—his friend began to use profanity and was disrespectful toward his family. Although his mother and father disapproved, what could they do? His friend was like a family member now. He taught Matt how to dress, how to act, and even how to treat others. Although his parents wouldn't admit it, he taught them a thing or two as well.

Once Matt reached his teen years, his friend's influence was obvious. Matt spent more time with him than with his family. Matt's dad and mom were always gone, so his friend taught him about life. He introduced Matt to alcohol, drugs, and pornography. He explained how sex before marriage wasn't a bad thing; everybody was doing it, even with same-sex partners. Surprisingly, Matt's parents allowed his friend to continue to live in their home. After all, they enjoyed his company; he was a great entertainer.

When Matt grew older, he realized that the friendship should never have continued. He believed that his friend's influence encouraged his dad's affair, his mom's problem with alcohol, and eventually, their divorce; the impact of Matt's friend on him was just as devastating.

Today, with full knowledge of the damage done, Matt still allows his friend to live with him, and, amazingly, he still listens to his advice. Matt's friend has a name; it's television.

Although fictitious, Matt's story is more fact than fiction; it's characteristic of so many homes today—**what goes in ultimately comes out.**

What amazed them amuses us

Just a few decades ago, most of today's television programs and movies would have shocked the public. Programs that never would have aired then, receive the highest ratings now.

 You may say, "Times change." And you are correct, but God's standards do not.

You may say, "Times change." And you are correct, but God's standards do not. The sin that once amazed us now amuses us. **When sin begins to amuse us, we are dangerously close to the edge:** "Woe to those who call evil good, and good evil" (Isaiah 5:20).

For those who doubt that there is a significant contrast between God's Word and what most entertainment and media outlets promote, the following may surprise you:

Media: Cheat on your spouse; everyone is doing it.
Truth: "Whoever commits adultery ... destroys his own soul" (Proverbs 6:32). Additionally, refer to Deuteronomy 5:18.

Media: Have sex before marriage; experiment with same-sex partners.
Truth: "Marriage is honorable among all, and the bed undefiled; but fornicators (sex outside of marriage) God will judge" (Hebrews 13:4). Additionally, see Romans 1:18-32.

Media: Abort your mistake; after all, it's only a fetus, not a baby.
Truth: "Before I formed you in the womb I knew you" (Jeremiah 1:5). Psalm 139:13 says, *God formed my inward parts; He knit me together in my mother's womb.* Clearly, life begins at conception. See Proverbs 6:17 and Deuteronomy 5:17.

Media: Party—eat, drink, and be merry for tomorrow we die.
Truth: "But take heed to yourselves, lest your hearts be weighed down with carousing, drunkenness, and cares of this life, and that Day [Jesus's return] come on you unexpectedly" (Luke 21:34).

Media: Cut corners and lie if that's what it takes to get ahead.

Truth: "The integrity of the upright will guide them" (Proverbs 11:3). "Such is the fate of all who are greedy for gain. It ends up robbing them of life" (Proverbs 1:19 NLT). Check out Deuteronomy 5:20 as well.

Media: Disrespect your parents and their out-dated advice.

Truth: "Honor your father and your mother, as the Lord your God has commanded you, that your days may be long" (Deuteronomy 5:16).

What most in the media promote and what the truth actually is are hardly compatible. No wonder families are disintegrating; it's evident to me that we've embraced an attitude of compromise in our nation, and, more sadly, in our homes. *Culture is religion externalized.* In other words, the culture around us simply reflects who and what we value. How we dress, what we view, who we hang out with, what we listen to, and how we spend our time, all speak volumes as to what we cherish. Are we cherishing the things of God, or the things of the world?

The battle within

The enemy rarely pushes us off the cliff, so to speak. *We're often led down one step at a time, one compromise at a time, one wrong choice at a time.* For example, the enemy doesn't show a young couple the pain and anguish and the years of regret that an abortion brings; he deceives them with the temporary enjoyment of premarital sex and a false sense of freedom from responsibility. If the full story was known beforehand, no doubt different choices might have

We're often not shown the pain that sin brings, we're enticed by the temporary pleasure.

been made. We're often not shown the pain that sin brings, we're enticed by the temporary pleasure.

Galatians 5:17 says that *the Spirit gives us desires that are opposite from what our sinful nature desires, and that these two forces are constantly fighting against each other.* As a result, our choices are rarely free from this conflict. In other words, our sinful nature and our new nature in Christ are constantly at war. Don't be alarmed. The fact that there is a fight confirms the value of our commitment. A paraphrase of, *The Battle Within,* found in my previous books, illustrates this truth:

A young man, determined to find help for his troubled life, walked to a neighboring church. He told the pastor that his life was meaningless and in constant turmoil. He wanted to make better choices, but couldn't.

He described the conflict: "It's as if I have two dogs constantly battling within me. One dog is evil, while the other is good. The battles are long and difficult; they drain me emotionally and mentally."

Without a moment's thought, the pastor asked, "Which dog wins the battles?" Hesitantly, the young man admitted, "The evil dog." The pastor looked at him and said, *"That's the one you feed the most. You need to starve that dog to death!"*

The pastor realized, as should we, that the source of our strength comes from the food that we choose. *What we feed grows, and what grows becomes the dominating force within our lives.* **Sin never stands still—it either grows or withers depending on whether you feed or starve it.**

Which dog wins the battle in your mind? Entertainment plays a huge role in this. Proverbs 23:7 says, *as a man thinks in his heart, so is he.* And Jesus said that *the lamp of the body is the eye. When your eye is good your body will be full of light. When your eye is bad your body will be full of darkness.* (Refer to Luke 11:34.) Our thoughts become words, our words become actions, our actions become habits. Who is shaping your thoughts? A daily diet of violence, lust, anger, and depression will fuel those very things in your life. One of the reasons why men and women struggle with lust or anger is because they feed those emotions continually throughout the day. It's difficult to avoid premarital sex and outbursts of anger while continually watching movies and TV programs that promote them. As a matter of fact, many cases of sexual violence can be traced directly back to pornography. What we embrace eventually embraces us. "The more we follow

... you should pay close attention to what you watch and listen to—the force controlling it ultimately controls you.

(See Ephesians 2:12)

that which is good, the faster and the further we shall flee from that which is evil" (Matthew Henry).[18]

Some may say that being cautious with what we view and listen to borders on legalism (e.g., performance-based religion). Although it can when taken to extremes, I disagree. Entertainment is not merely entertainment; depending on how it's used, it can be a very destructive influence. The Bible reveals that the devil is the prince of this world (Ephesians 2:2); therefore, you should pay close attention to what you watch and listen to—the force controlling it ultimately controls you. Romans 8:6 (NLT) states, "If your sinful nature controls your mind, there is death. But if the Holy Spirit controls your mind, there is life and peace." With God's help, you'll begin to control your thoughts instead of allowing your thoughts to control you.

For those who are skeptical about the media's influence, consider why companies spend millions of dollars on commercials. They obviously understand the concept of "suggestive selling."

In the end, the choice is yours when it comes to what you watch and listen to, but **why would you willingly walk into the enemy's camp?** Why would you feed wrong desires and thoughts when they do nothing but war against the soul? If you're questioning God's existence, experiencing violent bursts of anger, severely struggling with an addiction or lust, or continually feeling depressed or discouraged, evaluate your mental diet of television, movies, the Internet, music, friends, and your thoughts in general. Are they lifting you up, or pulling you down? There is no middle ground— you're being influenced one way or the other. Are there any changes that need to be made in your life? If so, this is where you start to win the battle within.

Begin your day by reading the Bible instead of watching television. While driving, try listening to thought-provoking sermons or praise and worship music. In the evenings, try praying and reading instead of browsing the Internet or watching television. Again, although this position may seem radical or extreme, we are living in extreme times. Our adversary never sleeps nor slumbers; his goal is to destroy our testimony, our character, and our soul if he can.

Being tempted isn't sin—surrendering to it is. Temptation is also an opportunity to do what is right by turning from it. I Corinthians 10:13 states, "No temptation has overtaken you except such as is common to man; but God is faithful, who will not allow you to be tempted beyond what you are able, but with the temptation will also make the way of escape, that you may be able to bear it." **The door of temptation swings both ways—you can enter or exit.** The key is to make choices that promote spiritual victory, not defeat.

To be honest, I once considered those who chose not to watch certain movies and television programs, or listen to certain music as fanatical or overly enthusiastic, even weird. *I now realize that if I don't control my desires, my desires will control me—right thinking creates right doing.* Years ago, after I recommitted my life to Christ, my craving for alcohol greatly increased at certain times. A week or two would pass and the desire to drink would again surface; sometimes I gave in to the desire. I quickly noted that every time I watched certain television programs, listened to suggestive music, and associated with the wrong crowd (a major trap), the desire to drink would increase significantly. I was convinced that if I wanted a healthy and fulfilling spiritual life, I would have to choose my mental food, as well as my friends, wisely. We'll never be completely free from wrong desires; there is a constant struggle to resist temptation, but, as we discussed earlier, there's a clear difference between a struggle and a lifestyle. Even Christ was tempted, but he was not drawn away by sin. God's Word anchored Him, and it will anchor us as we encounter the battles ahead.

 What was defined as pornography a few decades ago now fills our television screens on a nightly basis; what a sad testimony to the world.

Compromise—a very troubling trend

Let me begin by saying that I'm not writing this section, or the book for that matter, as if I have overcome all the challenges associated with being a Christian—nor do I want to approach this topic with a "holier than you" attitude, but to not be open and honest about this critical issue would be unwise and unbiblical. I also believe that, instead of continually bashing Hollywood, Christians should pray for the industry and seek to change the quality of the programming. Hollywood is a mission field that needs prayer more than protest.

Some time ago, I was disheartened to read an article in a major newspaper entitled: *"Values Message Vanishes on Tube."*[19] The article suggested that those who voted for President George W. Bush because of moral values apparently were not embracing those same values at home when considering what they viewed. What was defined as pornography a few decades ago now fills our television screens on a nightly basis; what a sad testimony to the world.

> **❝** *Where does Christianity destroy itself in a given generation? It destroys itself by not living in the light, by professing a truth it does not obey.* **❞**
>
> **—A.W. TOZER**

As W. Graham Scroggie said, "Light and darkness, right and wrong, good and evil, truth and error are incompatibles ... when they compromise it is the light, the right, the good, and the truth that are damaged."

The biggest danger to the evangelical Church is not false religion or atheism, but *compromise*; it has always been a tool of the enemy. When compromise occurs, we can have church growth but no depth; numbers, but no character; enormous buildings, but small hearts. We "play" Christian, but have the tendency to compromise everything that Christ stood for. We have riches, wealth, and prosperity, but neglect the weightier matters—love, mercy, and forgiveness. When compromise reigns, we can easily become insensitive, indifferent, ineffective, unforgiving, unloving, unmoved, and self-righteous. "Where does Christianity destroy itself in a given generation? It destroys itself by not living in the light, by professing a truth it does not obey" (Tozer). (See Revelation 2:1-29 & 3:1-22.)

It's never my goal to criticize fellow Christians. As a matter of fact, I'm extremely grateful for the many spiritual leaders and friends who have positively influenced me. There is, however, a very troubling trend toward moral compromise in the evangelical church. I've witnessed soft porn images on Christian websites, questionable movie clips during PowerPoint sermons, and youth pastors talk about their favorite sexually charged TV show with the youth—all under the guise of "relating" to the culture. Ironically, as I was finishing this section of the book, I attended a youth conference. Although the conference was for young women, there were male volunteers present as well. The conference speaker began by showing sexual images on the large screen in the church. These images were taken directly from music videos and magazines, and from CD and DVD covers. As I looked up, I saw a cross on one side of the building and a clip of a sexually explicit music video on the other. The speaker showed clip after clip of these images; she wanted to create shock value. Although she had a very good message and appeared extremely sincere, I believe that her message was compromised. It's hard to justify having the cross of Christ on one side of the church and those types of images on the other. In my opinion, the light, the right, the good, and the truth are damaged. **The church should not reflect or imitate the world, but lovingly confront it.** Psalm 101:3 warns us not to put anything wicked before our eyes, and I Timothy 4:12 exhorts us to be examples of purity and decency. *We do need to shock people; we need to shock them with the truth of God's Word.* In our pursuit to "relate to others," and to "reach people where they are," we run the risk of serving two masters. Like the Old Testament prophet, Elijah, who spoke on God's behalf, the same plea goes out today: *how long will you waiver between two opinions? If God is God, follow Him!* (Check out I Kings 18:20-46.)

This trend toward compromise is so troubling that I've included some of the prevailing views. The following pages contain five common comments that I've heard from

Christians. My thoughts follow each comment. Again, my intent is not to criticize; I've made many mistakes in this area as well. My comments are intended to challenge all of us. Although not shared by all, the following statements reflect the disturbing drift toward moral compromise. It leaves one to wonder: who's guiding Christians today—Hollywood or the Holy Spirit?

#1. *I was preached at for watching certain movies, listening to certain music, and for watching television—this really turned me off. We shouldn't tell people what to watch.*

Most of us can relate to this, but it should not be an excuse for watching and listening to very questionable material. Here's a helpful hint: before jumping to conclusions, try to determine if the person "preaching" is really offering "constructive" criticism. Many times, advice from parents or those in leadership, appears as criticism, when, in fact, they are acknowledging Proverbs 9:9, *teach the wise and they will be even wiser. Teach the righteous and they will learn even more.* Although difficult at times, maturity learns to embrace constructive criticism and to consider the advice of others. It's wise to first examine our lifestyle before condemning the messenger. "When God wants to speak and deal with us, he does not avail himself of an angel but of parents, or the pastor, or of our neighbor" (Martin Luther).

On the flip side, far too many of us have forgotten about *grace*. As a result, legalism surfaces; legalism has been known to condemn **all** music, movies, and television programs. *It can be defined as a self-righteous attitude that rates spirituality by how well a person follows rules.* A legalist often has a sliding scale mentality—the more

... we must learn to recognize what glorifies Christ and what clearly does not—then choose accordingly.

rules and regulations a person follows, the more spiritual he or she becomes. The legalist often forgets that we are saved because of what Christ did, not by what we do. He or she may have the tendency to view struggling Christians as counterfeits because they don't measure up to a certain standard. Most Christians will struggle with legalism from time-to-time, that's why it's important to discuss it, and avoid it.

It's been said that grace is one of the most misunderstood of all Christian doctrines. If abused, a person may continue in sin and see nothing wrong with it; if grace is neglected, one may never experience true freedom in Christ. A well-known pastor, Chuck Swindoll, once stated it this way: "The liberating truth about our freedom in Christ flies in the face of do-it-yourself religion and challenges Christ's followers who are enslaved to man-made rules and regulations to break free." He adds, "At the same time, grace promotes a powerful devotion to Christ and obedience to His Word, not to someone's guilt-giving list of DOs and DON'Ts."[20] That's the message that I hope to convey—some matters must be determined by an individual's own conscience. (See Romans 14:1-15.) However, we must learn to recognize what glorifies Christ and what clearly does not—then choose accordingly. **Grace does not relieve us of responsibility; we actually live under a higher standard when grace,**

To suggest that Jesus would "get with the times" and watch a sexually explicit music video or television program in order to "relate" to others, is unthinkable.

not rules, guides our decisions. Those who are living under grace won't want to continue in sin.

The bottom line about entertainment is this: when we give our hearts to Christ, read and study the Word, and allow the Holy Spirit to guide us, questionable entertainment should no longer amuse us; we have a different Spirit guiding us. The last half of Galatians 6:14 (NLT) states this well: "Because of that cross, my interest in this world died long ago, and the world's interest in me is also long dead." Romans 8:5 adds that *those who live according to their sinful nature set their minds on the things that excite that nature, but those who live according to the Spirit set their minds on what the Spirit desires.* **We are free to choose what we allow to enter into our minds—but if it begins to control us, we are no longer free, but bound.** (See I Corinthians 10:23.)

To be completely honest, the list of acceptable entertainment is small, very small. For some, the best policy may be *out of sight, out of mind.* You'd be amazed at what a week or two of no television would do for your spiritual life.

#2. *When television was first introduced to the public, many Christians complained. Now, sitcoms, music videos, and reality shows are the "bad" things. What's the big deal?*

Let's be careful not to make excuses and compromise God's Word in the name of entertainment. To suggest that Jesus would "get with the times" and watch a sexually explicit music video or television program in order to "relate" to others, is unthinkable. Let us not forget that cancer begins with a single cell. In time, this tiny cell consumes the life of the body. The full-blown moral crisis that we are experiencing today began with small compromises. Again, times change, but God's standards do not. But you may say, "Everyone is doing it—what's the big deal?" If everyone's doing it, take a second look. "The masses are always wrong. In every generation the number of the righteous is small. Be sure you are among them" (Tozer).[21]

Throughout the Bible we are commanded to remove anything that causes us to stumble—yes, *anything*. Again, this may sound as if it borders on legalism, and it can when taken to extremes. But when Paul addressed legalism in the second chapter of Colossians, for example, he zeroed in on festivals and Sabbath days, and on consuming, or not consuming, certain foods. Nowhere do we read in the Bible where legalism refers to being cautious with what we allow to enter our minds. **There is a clear difference between legalism and wisdom—legalism is of no value against the lust of the flesh; wisdom is.** King David said, "I will walk within my house with a perfect heart. I will set nothing wicked before my eyes" (Psalm 101:2-3). Although he failed at times, David was saying that integrity and moral uprightness should be pursued, especially in the home. **Being selective with what we watch and listen to has nothing to do with legalism; it has everything to do with spiritual integrity, wisdom, and moral purity.** Colossians 3:17 declares, *whatever you do in word or in deed, you should do to the glory of God.*

Again, pray for Hollywood; pray that Christian producers, executives, actors, and actresses bring Christian values to the set without compromise. We are beginning to see a glimmer of hope with the rise of the Independent Film Industry.

#3. *A Christian "has to" wear, listen to, and watch certain things. We need to break this cookie-cutter version of Christianity. We should show the attractive side of Christianity and not be so extreme.*

Although we definitely want to relate to others, our lifestyle should reflect our core convictions. This does not mean that we should be prudish and conceited, but real, humble, and loving. They'll know that we are Christians by our love and by our convictions, not by how well we imitate the world around us. I seldom hear non-Christians say, "I'm turned off by Christianity because my Christian friends are too selective with what they view and listen to," but I often hear, "Christians who say one thing and do another really turn me off." Guarding your mind isn't just a good idea, it's absolutely necessary when it comes to overcoming the battle within and preserving your testimony. *There's an enormous difference between witnessing and being a witness.* Aside from guarding ourselves, you never know who might be watching. **A compromised life sends a compromised message.** Proverbs 4:23 (NLT) states, "Above all else, guard your heart, for it affects everything you do." Everything? Yes, everything! What you think provides the framework for who you become. But be clear on this as well: don't think that because you struggle in this area that you do not have a relationship with Christ. We all struggle. The lack of holiness in a professing Christian's life does not necessarily mean that they don't have a relationship with Christ, as some may suggest. Salvation is *not* determined by a sliding scale. **The church does the most for the world when it is least like the world.** Did you catch that? Christians do the most for the world when they are the least like the world. One reason why Christianity does not appeal to society is not because it's unattractive in the truest sense of the word, but because society does not want the Christ that they see in many Christians. Removing the "cookie-cutter" example set forth in the Bible is not the answer; returning to it is. Remember what I referred to earlier: one of the most common questions on the minds of young adults today is, *why would we want Christ when we don't want the Christ that we see in others?*

Granted, the church was not created to manufacture Christians that look the same way and act the same way; it's our differences that make us unique. But we must also understand that being accepted and liked by others isn't necessarily an indicator that we are following Jesus's example; often rejection is. Jesus said, "Blessed are those who are persecuted for righteousness' sake, for theirs is the kingdom of heaven" (Matthew 5:10). And in II Timothy 3:12, the apostle Paul reveals that "all who desire to live godly in Christ Jesus will suffer persecution."

Don't get me wrong, legalism, spiritual arrogance, and religious bondage turn as many people away as does lukewarm living, but it's risky to show people one side of Christianity and not the other. Although salvation is a free gift from God, discipleship requires responsibility on our part. In our zeal to lead people to Christ, we often paint a false picture of discipleship, or water it down altogether. I don't want to make this issue with entertainment bigger than it is, but I also don't want to minimize it. Jesus didn't say, "Follow me and you won't have to change anything"; He said, *deny yourself, pick up your cross, and follow Me* (Matthew 16:24). Jesus wants us to understand what's involved when we follow Him. (Check out Luke 14:25-35.)

Oswald Chambers offers this perspective, "[Jesus] never pleaded, He never entrapped; He made discipleship intensely narrow, and pointed out certain things which could never be in those who followed Him."[22] Chambers also said, "The words of the Lord hurt and offend until there is nothing left to hurt and offend. **Jesus Christ has no tenderness whatever toward anything that is ultimately going to ruin a man in the service of God.**"[23]

To suggest that what we view and listen to is not important to God is to alter His word. We should be selective when it comes to entertainment. Once others see an authentic, committed relationship with Christ (although they may not admit it), they may begin to desire one as well.

To the statement: "Christians shouldn't be so extreme, or worry about what they wear," I agree that being too rigid

We have extreme snowboarding, extreme mountain biking, extreme motor-cross, extreme skateboarding, extreme makeovers, and so on. Why, then, can't we have an extreme love for holiness, purity, and God's Word?

is wrong, but so is being too flexible. The key is to look continually to God's Word for direction, and to listen to the inner promptings of the Holy Spirit. (In Chapter Seven, my wife, Morgan, wrote a brief section specifically to young women about this topic.)

We have extreme snowboarding, extreme mountain biking, extreme motor-cross, extreme skateboarding, extreme makeovers, and so on. Why, then, can't we have an extreme love for holiness, purity, and God's Word? *You won't find a Scripture that warns against being "too committed" to Christ.* We shouldn't feel that we have to act a certain way; we should want to. **A Christian should wear Christ on the inside as well as the outside.** Actions reflect the condition of the heart, from what we wear to what we view. As a tree is known by its fruit, we are known by our conduct, and thus, our choices.

#4. *Christians, especially preachers, spend way too much time trying to label what is good or bad, black or white, when it comes to entertainment; it makes for easy preaching.*

I tend to believe just the opposite. The truth is that we don't spend enough time teaching right from wrong. With some suggesting that less than 40 percent of "born-again" Christians believe in moral absolutes (it's considerably less among young adults), the need to address this topic has never been greater. How will we know the difference between right and wrong if it's not defined according to God's Word? King Solomon prayed for God to give him an understanding heart that he would be able to discern between good and evil. (Refer to I Kings 3:9.) The ability to "discern" between right and wrong is absolutely critical.

Unfortunately, the tendency is to tell young adults what they "want" to hear instead of what they "need" to hear. As a result, topics such as holiness, purity, and morality are often avoided. *We should be holy because He who called us is Holy* (I Peter 1:15). Holiness is not a strange, outdated word. It's being set apart, or separated from anything that causes us to sin, whether mentally (in what we think), or physically (in what we do). Holiness begins in the heart. We should continually strive for holiness in all that we do and say. "The Holy Spirit is first of all a *moral flame.* It is not an accident of language that He is called the *Holy* Spirit, for whatever else the word *holy* may mean it does undoubtedly carry with it the idea of moral purity."[24]

At this point you may think, "Wow, I could never measure up." Let me reassure you: God doesn't let our relationship with Him hinge on "measuring up," or on "following rules." He wants us to come as we are, recognize our need for a Savior, and commit our life to Him. **The key is to love God and people, and to make choices that reflect that love.** Remember … God's principles are guardrails through the canyons of life. They don't prevent us from enjoying life; they protect us from falling.

#5. *I don't worry about what I watch or listen to as long as my heart is right. Plus, I need to watch what everyone else is watching so I can relate to them.*

This is a very dangerous view. Most will admit, however, that this statement is really just an excuse to cross the line when it comes to entertainment. Let's be honest: many rationalize watching and listening to very questionable

If we would make it our goal to know Christ more personally, we would preach Christ more powerfully.

material not because they want to relate to others, but because they enjoy it.

What we watch and listen to affects the heart; it's impossible to separate the two. If we would make it our goal to know Christ more personally, we would preach Christ more powerfully. For example, if a pastor fills his mind with worldly pleasures and desires all week and expects the Spirit of God to speak boldly through him from the pulpit, he will be gravely mistaken. "The gratification of the flesh and the fullness of the Spirit do not go hand in hand" (R.A. Torrey). Who he is all week is who he will be when he steps to the pulpit—the passion and conviction of his message is only as strong as the passion and conviction within him. The same is true with you and me: "For out of the abundance of the heart the mouth speaks" (Matthew 12:34). What goes in ultimately comes out.

The Scriptures are crystal clear on the issue of entertainment; there's really no debate. Philippians 4:8 says *to fix our thoughts on what is true and honorable and right, and to think about things that are pure and lovely and admirable and worthy of praise.* Ephesians 5:1-20 also addresses this issue, and enough is said in II Timothy alone to silence any debate: *everyone who names the name of Christ should depart from anything that goes against His standard of holiness. We must be pure vessels that God can use.* (See II Timothy 2:19-21.) A pure vessel cannot come from a polluted mind. Years of feeding the flesh will leave us spiritually weak. James 1:27 reveals that Christians are to remain "unspotted" from the world; which literally means to be free from the world's corruption. **Are we "affecting" the world, or is the world "infecting" us?**

Again, it's not about following rules. Let your freedom in Christ, and a relationship with Him, guide you. We've all watched questionable material and have made wrong choices; don't live with ongoing regret. But don't justify wrong behavior by thinking that God doesn't care about what you watch or listen to, because He does; we serve and love God with our mind. (See Romans 7:25 and Luke 10:27.) What we view and listen to clearly affects our relationship with Him. If we find dozens of hours a week to watch movies and television programs, but have little time for God, our relationship with Him will suffer—period.

Drawing the line

Years ago, I realized that if I wanted to grow spiritually, some things would have to go, or, at the very least, be minimized; I needed to draw a line. Instead of watching hours of television a day, I began to devote my time to activities that strengthened my relationship with the Lord. I cannot begin to tell you how much of a difference that made. Although far from perfect, I began to put first things first. As a result, I began to

It's impossible to develop a deep respect and desire for God if we repeatedly fill our mind with things that oppose Him.

hunger for God's Word and spiritual truth like never before. It's impossible to develop a deep respect and desire for God if we repeatedly fill our mind with things that oppose Him.

When it comes to drawing a line between healthy entertainment and a destructive influence, follow Christ rather than the crowd. Granted, sometimes it's difficult to know which movies and programs to avoid, but you can think ahead and decide what the outcome will be. Oswald Chambers suggests: "Push it to its logical conclusion, and if the outcome is something that God would condemn, allow it no more ... ."[25] Research the *content* beforehand rather than the rating. There are online movie review websites that highlight questionable material, use them, but keep in mind that there are no hard and fast rules. I know people who won't watch any R-rated movies, and I know others who just avoid movies with excessive sexual content, and/ or extreme violence. I have my boundaries as well. **Liberty has limits—the key is to ask, "Will it build me up spiritually, or pull me down?"** In gray areas, each person will have their own convictions—allow them that freedom.

Depending on the circumstance, you may be confronted with a challenging decision from time to time. A friend of mine was asked to go to the movies with her family because a relative, visiting from out of town, was leaving the next day. Although the movie was not one that she would have chosen, my friend went. Had she said, "Sorry, I'm a Christian; I can't go," her family would have been hurt, as well as upset. This does not mean that we should always compromise our standards to relate to others; I merely shared this as one example among many. Because of my friend's non-threatening relationship with her family, she has been able to share Christ with them.

Let me leave you with this thought: if you are a young adult, are you willing to do what it takes to protect your mind and your relationship with the Lord? If you are a parent, are you willing to do what it takes to protect your family? It's your choice. Drawing a line can be out of step with the mainstream, but, like Joshua, we too must say: *choose this day whom you will serve, as for me and my house we will serve the Lord* (Joshua 24:15).

Embrace 'grace'

Compassion and understanding with others should be our motives when approaching the topic of entertainment; it's often not *what* we say but *how* we say it that matters. Admittedly, I've failed in this area because I did not embrace grace at opportune times. We should not excuse sin and become tolerant—offering grace does not mean that we approve of sinful behavior, but it does mean that we are sensitive to those within our sphere of influence. The only command that Jesus gave the woman caught in the act of adultery was *to go and sin no more* (John 8:11). He rebuked the sin, not the sinner. He didn't condemn or criticize her. He allowed compassion and grace to guide His words. We should seek to do the same.

To aspiring leaders, and those in positions of leadership: we must proclaim God's Word without watering down the message. *It's been said that people don't care how much we know until they know how much we care.* Love and grace should be the driving forces behind our message, not winning arguments. Instead of concentrating on how far someone still needs to go spiritually, concentrate on how far they've come. An attitude of constant criticism is not a "positive character trait"; it often reveals an inner drive to exalt oneself. Get rid of it. Among other things, love is patient and kind, not rude or critical; it protects not attacks. We must speak the truth, but be patient when others do not agree. *There are times to create conflict, times to resolve it, and times to avoid it—use discernment.* (See Proverbs 27:6.) I can think of instances when I shared something with someone that initially upset them, but they later thanked me. I can think of other times when I should have said nothing. We all make mistakes, and a "holier than you" attitude is not the right approach. **Although very challenging at times, I'd rather err on the side of grace than on the side of judgment.**

In a booklet by Chuck Swindoll entitled, *It's Time to Embrace Grace,* he lists several ways to minister grace to others; here are just a few:

I. Accept others, and let them be. If you disagree on matters of conscience, such as [certain] movies or style of worship, remain silent. Just accept those around you, and throw away that list of things people have to do before you'll be convinced that they're spiritual.

II. Refuse to dictate to those around you. In matters of conscience where Scripture is silent, refuse to convince others that your way is right. You may feel compelled to tell others your convictions and then require them to follow your guidelines. But where's the grace in that?

III. Free others from your judgment. Because we will all stand before God, the role of judge is already filled. Once we have clearly proclaimed the truth in matters clearly defined by Scripture, our job is finished ... We don't know all the facts. We don't know the scars and pain of their pasts. We don't know the heartaches they've had to grow through and get beyond ... God tells us to leave justice to Him.

> *" True Christianity, where it reigns in the heart, will make itself appear in the purity of life. "*
>
> **—ISAAC WATTS**

IV. Love others. If you enjoy seeing a respectable movie at the theater, great! Just don't chide the one who's convinced Christians have no business funding Hollywood. When you embrace grace, you intentionally avoid flaunting your liberty ... When you love one another you work on ways to keep from hurting your brothers and sisters in Christ. [26]

We must strive to balance God's grace with His commandments, and look to Christ as our example. "True Christianity, where it reigns in the heart, will make itself appear in the purity of life" (Isaac Watts).[27]

In closing, there will be those who won't understand your stance and strong convictions; you may "appear" arrogant or self-righteous; this cannot always be prevented. There is an enormous difference between what others may mistake for conceit and self-righteousness in you, and a strong commitment to God's Word. Without one word from you, they may feel convicted because of your lifestyle. After I became a Christian, I lost most of my friends (this was a good thing). Most felt that I was "high-minded" simply because I embraced a new standard for my life. Don't let the pressure and negative opinions of others draw you away from God's call to a higher standard. *If you do feel holier than others, remove that attitude—you are only forgiven. All of us are in the process of being transformed, and this begins with humility.*

Questions to consider for Chapter Four:

1. Why is it dangerous to allow sin to amuse us? Are there any areas where you regularly compromise? As you reflect, keep this statement in mind: thoughts become words, words actions, actions habits, and habits shape your lifestyle.

2. If how we dress, what we view, who we hang out with, what we listen to, and how we spend our time, speak volumes as to what we cherish, are we cherishing the things of God, or the things of the world?

3. Galatians 5:17 reveals that the Spirit gives us desires that are opposite from what our sinful nature desires, and that these two forces are constantly fighting against each other. How can you make choices that feed the spirit rather than the flesh?

4. What we watch and listen to affects the heart; it's impossible to separate the two. If we would make it our goal to know Christ more personally, we would share Christ more powerfully. How can you make it a point to know Christ more personally?

5. Even though it's very challenging at times, would you rather err on the side of granting grace or being judgmental? What are some simple ways you can show grace to others?

Recommended Reading:
The Strategy of Satan by Warren W. Wiersbe
T.V.: The Great Escape by Bob DeMoss
The Root of the Righteous by A.W. Tozer
The Chuck Swindoll Collection by Chuck Swindoll
Battle Cry for a Generation by Ron Luce is another exceptional resource; it offers statistics and additional information regarding the media's influence on today's culture.

The quality of your choice today will affect the quality of your life tomorrow.

———————

It's primarily a person's character, not their looks, that determines success or failure in a relationship.

CHAPTER FIVE

FINDING
Mr. or Miss Right

Set the brake!

YOU MAY HAVE READ THE TITLE OF THIS CHAPTER in the front of the book and skipped ahead to this topic, but I strongly encourage you to resist the tendency to skip ahead. Each preceding chapter is important and relevant; they lay the groundwork necessary for this chapter. With that said, let's begin.

Although it was years ago, I remember it as if it was yesterday—largely because it was one of the most embarrassing moments of my life. When I was seventeen, I drove my old Chevy Blazer to my father's construction yard. I parked and walked toward his office. I looked back only to find my truck following me as it gained speed. Before I could stop it, the truck slammed into a block wall. Although little damage was done to the truck, I was humiliated. My dad and several of his friends were there. The first words out of my father's mouth were, "Did you set the parking brake?" Hesitantly, I replied, "No."

Days earlier, my dad reminded me to always set the parking brake until he could find out why the transmission wasn't holding. I remembered a very important lesson that day: **knowledge is knowing what to do; wisdom is doing it; both are important.** I knew what to do; I just didn't do it. I once heard that knowledge knows that a snowball is flying at your face—wisdom ducks. Hopefully, this chapter will encourage you to make wise decisions when it comes to dating, and ultimately marriage. "Wisdom and knowledge will be the stability of your times" (Isaiah 33:6).

Michelle ... and so many more

There was a young woman; let's call her Michelle. Michelle began dating Mark when she was 16. He told her that he was also a Christian and that he respected her standards. He mentioned that he had been sexually active in the past, but that he felt differently about her. He reassured her that it wouldn't happen in their relationship. The fact that he had been involved intimately with other girls bothered Michelle, but she wanted to believe him, and he was very attractive.

As they continued to date, Mark's influence was strong. Michelle stopped attending church and youth group. She also lost interest in reading her Bible and praying. As a result, her relationship with Christ was no longer a priority.

 If the person you're dating seems like "a nice person," give it time, a lot of time, before truly coming to that conclusion.

Eventually, Mark convinced Michelle to spend the night, and she gave in to his sexual advances. The following morning she was devastated. Her only comfort was in believing that Mark loved her, especially now, and would marry her. She was wrong. Within a few months, Mark was gone, and Michelle was emotionally shattered. She had given away the gift that she had resolved would be given to only one person. In addition, she was pregnant.

What can we learn from Michelle's experience? Although these points focus primarily on Michelle's choices, Mark's list of irresponsible actions is just as long. Can you spot them?

> Michelle overlooked Mark's major character flaws because she liked how he "looked" and made her "feel." It's primarily a person's inner qualities, not their outer features that determine success or failure in a relationship. Outer beauty is fleeting, but inner qualities endure. Take away the body, and what do you have? If you marry, in time, that body will change, and you'll want to be happy with the person inside.

> Although Mark said that he felt differently about Michelle, she should have regarded his actions rather than his words. His past sexual experiences and failure to truly repent and change should have been clear warning signs. Mark's personal agenda manipulated Michelle; he told her what she wanted to hear. *Remember, actions speak louder than words.* Most are on their best behavior while dating because they only want a sexual relationship. It's usually not until after marriage that major flaws begin to surface. If the person you're dating seems like "a nice person," give it time, a lot of time, before truly coming to that conclusion. **Selfishness, not godly character, drives the actions of many today.**

> Michelle's relationship with Mark distracted her from God. Rather than continuing to grow spiritually, she invested more time in Mark and other activities. *She should have followed wholeheartedly after Christ and watched to see if Mark kept up.*

> When Mark asked Michelle to spend the night, he revealed his motives, no guesswork here. The enemy didn't push Michelle off the edge; he took her down one step at a time, one compromise at a time, and one mistake at a time.

> Michelle thought that she would someday marry Mark. This false assumption allowed Mark to edge his way into her heart. Michelle should have guarded her heart and realized that sex before marriage was not an option.

> When Michelle separated herself from God's protection, she had two choices: to *fall backward* or to *fall forward*. If she chose to fall forward into God's forgiveness, in time, God's grace would heal and restore her. Many, like Michelle, have abandoned hope of ever being accepted because of past sexual sin. **Don't lose hope ... God wants you to** *fall forward* **into His arms, not away.**

If this story rings true in your life, you can also ask for forgiveness, change your lifestyle, and position yourself once again in the center of God's will. It's important to feel convicted and sorry about sin, and to repent (repentance allows us to see sin as God sees it). The danger comes when a hardness of heart prevents us from turning to God.

Caution—regret ahead

References to sexual experiences in the Bible are sometimes defined with statements such as, "He knew

... if the person you're dating is not concerned with purity, reconsider the relationship.

his wife." To *know*, in this context, is to know intimately through a sexual experience. Regrettably, for those who experience sex before marriage, it's impossible to un-know what is known. Think about that: sexual experiences cannot be un-done. Each time we engage in premarital sex, we add emotional weight to our lives. It's difficult to run a marital marathon while carrying the extra weight of regret from past relationships. Sex is good and God-ordained, but only in the context of marriage between a man and a woman. That's how God designed it.

In Matthew 18:7, Jesus had harsh words for those who influence others to rebel against God's design. He said, *although we live in a sinful world, woe be to the man through whom the sin comes.* In other words, if you're manipulating situations and people to fulfill sexual desires, you will be held accountable for your actions. Men ... we are called to be the leaders in the relationship. Don't place the burden of leadership on the one that you are dating; demonstrate self-control in the area of sex. When we do this, we compliment her as someone of great value and respect.

A word of caution: *if the person you're dating is not concerned with purity, reconsider the relationship.* If they are not concerned with doing what's right now, they may not be concerned about doing what is right later. **The person who is not faithful to God may not be faithful to you.** Although they may find you attractive, their motivation to please God and protect your purity should outweigh their motivation for sex. If it doesn't ... you fill in the blank.

Unmistakably, the quality of your choice today will affect the quality of your life tomorrow. **If you desire a good marriage, or a fulfilled single life in the future, it begins with the right choice today.** When you choose to postpone sexual intimacy, despite your past, it will be worth the wait. Ask yourself, "Do I want to experience the temporary pain of discipline or the lasting pain of regret?"

If you're currently involved in a sexual relationship, understand that it's not where God wants you to be. He will not bless a sexually active lifestyle, but He can bless a choice to abstain until marriage. *When God brings a spouse, it's often when we're moving in the right direction, not the wrong one.*

Should I date or court?

Is there a difference between dating and courting? Some say that dating provides opportunities to spend time together and suggests that it can be short or long-term. Courting infers a long-term commitment with marriage in mind. Today's secular dating practices, largely encouraged by the media, focus on "hooking up" and fulfilling sexual desires. The goal should be to build a strong, meaningful relationship and to do what is right instead of labeling the relationship. God desires an exchange of respect, honesty, and self-control. *The term used isn't as important as the character demonstrated during the process.* (Refer to I Thessalonians 4:1-8.)

Regardless of whether you choose to date or court, consider these points:

- Don't rush the relationship; allow it to grow at a healthy pace.

- Share the same spiritual beliefs; be equally yoked. This is crucial!

- Initially, spend only a day or two a week together; slowly add more time. Don't become emotionally attached—keep other interests alive.

- When possible, date in public and/or in the company of friends and family.

- Ask others for input, especially from those who know the character of the other person.

- Avoid discussing future plans such as marriage or children too soon.

- Avoid making decisions based solely on emotions.

- Occasionally, take a week away from the relationship. Allow time to think as you seriously seek God's will for the relationship.

- Guard your speech. Don't say things that may stimulate premature desires.

- Set boundaries, and avoid situations that fuel sexual desire. The power of touch, for example, creates incredible feelings. God designed this to be shared within its proper context. Mistakenly, many view dating or courting as a license to touch without restriction.

- Ask, "Does God want me to be in a relationship at this particular time in my life?" In my opinion, it's best to avoid dating just for the sake of dating. There's nothing wrong with waiting for God's best. *Do not awaken love until the time is right* (Song of Solomon 2:7).

This list may sound extreme, but extreme or not, failed relationships start with compromise. It's been estimated that

"Christian" marriages and secular marriages now share the same divorce rate. Whether true or not, one wrong choice leads to another, and another. Recall what was said earlier: *if you don't control your desires, your desires will control you.*

Sex should distinguish marriage from all other relationships. A marriage that is firmly anchored creates a stable environment in which to raise children and sustain commitment. Sexual intimacy was not designed to be a recreational sport; it was intended to create a spiritual bond that would assure that "the two shall become one," and remain as one. In his book, *Love for a Lifetime,* Dr. James Dobson includes this powerful point: "Bonding refers to the emotional covenant that links a man and woman together for life and makes them intensely valuable to one another. It is the specialness that sets those two lovers apart from every other couple on the face of the earth."[28]

Although our pasts were less than ideal, had my wife and I had sex with one another before marriage, we would have lost something that God designed for us to share only as a married couple. We may have ended the relationship due to mistrust. Our commitment to wait until marriage, regardless of past mistakes, brought us to a new level of trust and respect. It's sobering to think that my loving wife may have been a past regret had we compromised in this area. This isn't to say that some couples can't have a happy marriage if they've had sex before marriage, but God wants to spare us the added pain and disappointment that comes with living in disobedience.

Take dating and courting seriously. If you respect and honor the person, you'll either gain a godly spouse or learn something from the experience. However, if you misuse His gift, a potential spouse may, instead, become a past regret.

" How far do you want your future spouse to have gone in his or her previous relationships— that's how far you should go! **""**

How far is too far?

Another frequently asked question is, "When it comes to sex, how far is too far?" One opinion that appears common is this: *when we become sexually stimulated either physically, or mentally, we begin to sin; our behavior is borderline.* At that point, we should take Paul's advice in I Corinthians 6:18, and "flee sexual immorality." **Flee is the key. But, it's hard to flee from what you feed.** If you frequently feed sexual desires by what you watch and listen to, fleeing will be difficult, if not impossible. The motivation to follow God's direction must outweigh the desire for sexual pleasure.

Joseph, an Old Testament figure, when confronted with adultery, ran from his boss's wife and said, "How then can I do this great wickedness, and sin against God?" He didn't say that he wasn't attracted to her; he said, "How can I sin against God!" His motivation to serve God was the key to his success, as is ours. (Check out Genesis 39.)

I once heard someone say, "How far do you want your future spouse to have gone in his or her previous relationships—that's how far you should go!" Don't take chances. If it feels like temptation, it probably is. Treat others with dignity and respect by not causing them to sin; they may some day be your spouse.

I encourage you to enlist an accountability couple, or a person who you can communicate with on a regular basis.

Prior to marriage, my wife and I talked often with trusted friends who would ask the difficult questions. Love is not only impatient at times, but blind as well; so seek feedback from those you trust. Invite them to share their thoughts about the relationship from their perspective; this can be a tremendous help. Proverbs 15:22 says that our plans can go wrong simply because we fail to ask for godly advice. Those who counsel us can generally offer guidance and make correct observations about the relationship; whereas, we might be inclined to lean on our emotions. But be careful: from time to time, you might be tempted to find someone to confirm your feelings. You may ask co-workers or friends for advice until you hear what you want to hear and not necessarily what you need to hear. **If the truth has to be altered to make the relationship appear better than it is, re-think the relationship.** When we are honest and open, others can make an accurate assessment of the relationship.

I've included a section at the end of this chapter entitled: *Questions to consider before marriage—how well do you know the other person?* This list will help you define expectations and learn as much as possible about each other. Although marriage may be years away, and some of

❝ If there is one single reason why many are unable to break the power of sexual sin ... [it's because] they have not made a radical commitment to holiness in every area of their lives. **❞**

—ERWIN W. LUTZER

... many of us fall back into sin because we're too close to the edge.

the questions may not be appropriate for all couples, it's still wise to review the list and gain insight before you marry.

Too close to the edge

If the largest factor contributing to the destruction of many young lives is the lack of sexual purity, why do so many continue to fall in this area? Here's a simple illustration that I heard some time ago. A young boy kept falling out of his bed week after week until his mother discovered that he was falling because he wasn't moving far enough in. In the same way, *many of us fall back into sin because we're too close to the edge.* We don't move far enough in to God's shelter of safety and protection. Pastor Erwin W. Lutzer said it best: "If there is one single reason why many are unable to break the power of sexual sin ... [it's because] they have not made a radical commitment to holiness in every area of their lives."[29] I couldn't agree more. **It's hard to get hit by a train if you're not on the tracks.**

Overcoming sin, especially sexual sin, can be a difficult battle for Christians. On one hand, the apostle Paul declares, "Our old sinful selves were crucified with Christ so that sin might lose its power in our lives" (Romans 6:6 NLT); yet, in the next chapter he states, *the good that I want to do, I don't do; but the evil I don't want to do, I end up doing* (Romans 7:19). It leaves one to wonder, "If I'm dead to sin, why is it still alive in me?" It's alive because *whatever we "choose" to obey becomes our master* (Romans 6:16). We can choose to sin, or we can choose to walk away. This may seem foreign, but it's not foreign to God. We need only to look at all the brokenness in the world to see that God's way is the best way.

Sin is present in this world, but its power over us is broken when we place our trust in Christ. The question is, "Do you position yourself to be drawn away by the strong pull of sin, or do you anchor yourself on solid ground?" The Bible contains strong warnings against any sexual activity outside of marriage. No matter how many laws are passed in favor of same-sex marriage, it will not change God's view. God cannot change His mind: *I am the Lord thy God—I change not* (Malachi 3:6); yet, the goal of some is to justify homosexuality, adultery, and pre-marital sex. It's been said that if you tell a lie long enough, and often enough, people will begin to believe it. And isn't that true.

On that note, let's briefly discuss the issue of homosexuality. Christians have erred on two extremes. On one extreme are those who insult, or who are violent toward, those trapped in this lifestyle; homosexuality appears at the top of their sin list. These people have a distorted truth and no love. The other extreme excuses this sin, looks the other way, and often ordains clergy who embrace it. They have distorted love and no truth. So what's the answer? Biblically speaking, a homosexual *lifestyle* is a prohibited sexual sin that's morally wrong and harmful. We should have compassion for those who are enslaved, but at the same time, we should not condone or excuse this type of sin any more than we condone or excuse any other sin such as adultery or fornication.[30]

While past sexual experiences cannot be reversed, our minds and spirits can be renewed and restored. Don't concentrate on perfection, or isolate yourself from others, but begin by asking God for guidance and strength as you face tough decisions. He'll place people in your life who can help you along the way. **Instead of concentrating on how far you have to go spiritually, concentrate on how far you've come.** Let that thought motivate you. Although your past, like most, may be marked by sexual sin, God's Word can bring healing. Don't allow past mistakes to cause future pain. If God is calling you back to a place of purity and wholeness, don't become discouraged because of past failure; recognize that *those who have been forgiven much, can love much* (Luke 7:47). "As far as the east is from the west, so far has He removed our transgressions from us" (Psalm 103:12).

Is there only one person for me?

When it comes to marriage, is there only one person for you? I don't have a clear-cut answer but the parable found in Luke 19:11-27 may offer insight. In a nutshell, a master gave his servants talents to invest but did not tell them where or how to invest them. Two of the servants invested wisely and took care of what had been given to them. The last servant hid the talent and did nothing with it. As a result, he lost it. We, too, are equally entrusted with gifts and freedom with how we are to invest, whether financially, relationally, or physically. Ultimately, we decide what to do with our gifts and responsibilities. Some may even have the gift of singleness; yes, it's a gift; ask those who are happily single, or unhappily married.

If you are seeking God wholeheartedly and are praying for a godly spouse, I believe that He will direct your steps, but in His time. Whether it's singleness or marriage—God

He stresses patience; we want it now. He wants to prepare us; we think we're ready. He wants to train us; we want to do it our way.

will reward you as you seek and honor Him. He stresses patience; we want it now. He wants to prepare us; we think we're ready. He wants to train us; we want to do it our way. He wants what's best for us; we'll take second best. **He wants to mold us into His image; we're more concerned with self-image.**

Unfortunately, relationships are often all about us. We fail to recognize that there is a Master Builder who has a master plan. Don't rush the process and waste time by trying to "find" someone. When we rush, we bring unneeded anxiety into our lives. **It's difficult to wait for Mr. or Miss "Right," because we want Mr. or Miss "Right Now."** More important than learning how to find Mr. or Miss Right, is learning how to become Mr. or Miss Right. Dating is not only about attracting the opposite sex; it's about attracting the right qualities in others.

The question really shouldn't be, "Is there only one person for me?" but rather, "Am I leading the life that God wants me to lead in order that I receive His best?" If one desires to find a trustworthy and committed person, he or she must also offer those qualities. This is the principle of *sowing* and *reaping.* Today, character qualities such as honesty, integrity, commitment, perseverance, and serving are almost non-existent. As a result, marriages are failing, families disintegrating, and relationships ending, simply because of self-centeredness.

In my case, as I was praying for a godly wife, God, through His Word, revealed areas in my own life that needed improvement. I would sometimes say, "I'll work on those areas, but in the meantime I'm looking for a spouse!" My attitude was wrong. *He wanted my first priority to be self-improvement, rather than self-fulfillment.* It's acceptable to pray for what we want with right motives, but we also need to pray that God will mold us into the person that He wants us to be—**who we are often determines who we'll attract.**

Finding God's best

The account of Abraham's servant who sought a wife for Abraham's son, Isaac, offers wonderful insight in defining our role in the pursuit of finding God's best for our lives. Although many books and sermons have highlighted this account, here are a few key points to consider. (Refer to Genesis 24:2-51.)

I. Seek in places pleasing to the Lord.

Abraham's servant was told where to find a wife for Isaac. He didn't visit those places that might parallel our nightclubs, parties, and online chat rooms; he followed the instruction to go back to his homeland and find a wife. He understood the principle: **where you look is what you'll find.** Abraham wanted a wife for his son who knew the Lord, so he said to his servant: *swear that you will not let my son marry a local Canaanite woman. Go to my homeland and find a wife for my son Isaac.* Abraham wanted Isaac to marry someone who shared his beliefs. Had Isaac married a Canaanite, he may have easily embraced their false gods and been led astray. In

It's easy to believe that you can influence the other person, especially once married, but they often have the leverage and can pull you down.

this, Abraham also teaches the principle discussed earlier of being equally yoked. (See II Corinthians 6:14.)

If you are standing on a wall, it's easier to be pulled down than to pull another up. Companions, good or bad, will influence you. It's easy to believe that you can influence the other person, especially once married, but they often have the leverage and can pull you down. (See I Kings 11:1-11.) Again, if the person you are dating doesn't have the qualities you're looking for, don't lower your standards, keep them high. On the flip side, don't be unrealistic with your expectations either.

Although Abraham lived in the city with unbelievers, he did not want his son to be married to one. We, too, should seek in places pleasing to the Lord. **We should "position" ourselves to receive God's best by "placing" ourselves in places that please Him.** For instance, Spring Break in Cancun and the Las Vegas party scene, are probably not good places to find a future spouse. Granted, we should not always be on the lookout for a spouse—the Lord knows our need; He'll provide in His time, but we should avoid places that attract the wrong crowd and pull us down spiritually.

II. Enter the relationship intending to give, not take. We read in verse 10 that *the servant loaded Abraham's camels with gifts.* The servant went out prepared to be a blessing. When you enter into a relationship, determine to be a blessing. Today's culture tends to ask, "What can I get from this relationship?" rather than, "What can I give to this relationship?" Enter the relationship with things such as honesty, integrity, and moral purity. When you give, ultimately you receive.

III. Prayer often precedes the blessing.
Next, we read in verse 15, *as he was praying, a young woman named Rebekah arrived.* Prayer preceded the blessing. As it is with us, prayer is often the key that unlocks the blessings in our lives. If we don't ask, we may not receive.

IV. Despite your past, strive for purity.
Verse 16 identifies Rebekah as a virgin. A desire for sexual purity is fundamental in finding the right person or being found by the right person. We may not understand why at the time, but God does not give meaningless directives. Often, you won't understand some of God's commands until you begin to obey them—obedience leads to wisdom. Had Rebekah had previous sexual encounters, although we don't know for sure, Abraham's servant may not have been led to her. She might have missed God's best for her life. **Despite your past, the desire to remain sexually pure until marriage must be at the top of your list.** I cannot stress this enough. Regardless of your past, God redeems.

V. Observe the attitudes and behaviors of the other.
Verse 21 states that *the servant watched her and remained silent, wondering whether or not she was the one.* In deciding whether to date or to continue dating, take time and observe the attitudes and behaviors of the other person. Are they inclined to serve, or to be served? Are they critical, argumentative, or defensive? Give yourself

time to observe their disposition, and remember that most will be on their best behavior, at least initially. Observe them around their family, children, when under pressure, and when upset. Also observe how a son treats his mother and a daughter her father as an indicator of potential strengths and weaknesses.

When I first noticed my wife in church, I watched how she treated others as well as how she dressed (e.g., modestly or alluring). I watched to see if she brought a new guy to church every Sunday, and I observed her attitude while at church—was she there for the right reason? Was she there to truly learn and grow, or was it simply a social outing? She was cautious with me as well. This was a tremendous help in taking steps toward a serious relationship. If you have concerns about the person that you're dating, it may be wise to postpone a relationship. *If you notice red flags such as substance abuse, violent or cruel behavior, persistent dishonesty, cheating, or severe problems with lust, it's probably time to end the relationship.*

VI. Be appreciative. Once the servant knew that he had found the right person, he thanked God and praised Him. How many times do we forget to thank God for guiding and leading us? We should constantly thank Him and ask for His continued direction in our lives.

If only we were as careful as Abraham's servant! In summary, we might say: spend time in places that please the Lord, choose one who shares your beliefs, bless others, pray, remain pure, be observant, be thankful, and remember, it's never too late for a new beginning. The only command Jesus gave the woman caught in the act of adultery was *to go and sin no more* (John 8:11). He didn't condemn her, criticize her, or bring up the past; He gave her clear direction concerning what to do from that point forward. **It's best to find yourself in the arms of God, redeemed, than to live broken outside of His will.** Which way will you run?

A quick tip about singleness

If you are unfulfilled as a single, the problem may be that you haven't been following God's plan for singleness. Being single isn't about living life on hold until you meet someone—it's about living life to the fullest even if you don't. The time spent while single is invaluable. Yes, there are occasions when we feel lonely and want a partner, but those feelings should not control our lives. During my single years, I had a strong desire for marriage, but I didn't put my life on hold. I wrote my first book, half of another, started three other titles, and designed a website. In addition, I studied the Bible regularly, listened to countless hours of sermons, read dozens of Christian books, and worked in construction. Without a doubt, it was a very productive time of my life. As a matter of fact, I could not have done it all while married. I Corinthians 7:32-33 (NLT) motivated me during that time: "An unmarried man can spend his time doing the Lord's work and thinking how to please him. But a married man can't do that so well. He has to think about his earthly responsibilities and how to please his wife." Although this applies to marriage,

Being single isn't about living life on hold until you meet someone—it's about living life to the fullest even if you don't.

dating can also prevent us from pursuing God if we are too captivated by the other person. **Don't view singleness as a burden, but a blessing. Being single can allow you to accomplish more, not less.**

Questions to consider before marriage—
How well do you know the other person?

Even if you are not planning to marry for some time, it's best to define your expectations now and to learn as much as you can before making one of the biggest decisions of your life. For example, can you see the person that you are dating or courting as the life-long mother or father of your children? Will they be someone you can respect years down the road? Will they be someone who remains committed to the marriage and to God, even through difficult times? It's very important to ask these types of questions beforehand. Unfortunately, many couples know little about each other before they marry; therefore, I've included this simple checklist.

Whose responsibility is it to ...
   1. Balance the finances?
   2. Earn an income?
   3. Pay the bills?
   4. Clean the house?
   5. Oversee household and automobile repairs?
   6. Do laundry?
   7. Cook dinner?
   8. Empty the trash?
   9. Help the kids with homework?

Add other responsibilities for discussion.

General questions:
   1. Will both of you work?

2. If both work, who cares for the children when they arrive?
3. How many children would you like to have?
4. How do you define your role as a parent?
5. Will you home-school your children, pay for private schooling, or enroll them in a public school? Why?
6. What church will you attend, and why?
7. Do you prefer to live in the city or the country?
8. Describe an ideal vacation.
9. How do you spend holidays and birthdays?
10. How do you spend weekends?
11. How much time should you spend together? How much time apart?
12. How is your attitude in general (e.g., defensive, passive, aggressive, compliant, resistant, etc.)?
13. As your parents age, will you place them in a home, or care for them yourself?
14. How will you manage your money? Will there be a budget?
15. Will you tithe, and/or give to others in need? How will you determine the amount?
16. Are you a saver or a spender?
17. Do you agree to discuss all topics openly and honestly?
18. What hurts your feelings in private? What about in public?
19. How long should a couple date and/or court before they marry? How long should the engagement last?
20. What might be your greatest challenge in marriage? Why?
21. What family traditions do you hold dear?

22. Do you like to entertain?

23. Do you like crowds, company, or visitors? Discuss various situations.

24. How will your views on politics affect the relationship? Which political party do you support? Why?

25. What are your feelings on topics such as abortion, embryonic stem-cell research, and same-sex marriage? Discuss other controversial issues.

(Note: If the relationship begins to move toward marriage, topics such as STDs and sexual problems should be discussed.)

Can you think of other questions?

Describe your family experiences. Discuss ...

1. Your early years.
2. Your father's role/your mother's role.
3. What you learned from your childhood experience.
4. Other experiences that you would like to discuss.
5. How your childhood was overall.
6. How you view life overall.
7. If and when you committed your life to Christ. Discuss your experience.
8. Your most painful memories/the happiest times in your life.
9. What you will do like your mother; like your father?
10. How you will be unlike your mother; unlike your father? How can you apply what you have learned from both of their lives?

Questions to consider for Chapter Five:

1. Do you agree that it's primarily a person's character, not their looks, that determines success or failure in a marriage, especially through times of adversity? If so, why do so many people overlook this fact? How can you be different?

2. When Michelle separated herself from God's presence, she had two choices: to fall backward, or to fall forward. How could she have *fallen forward*? Why are those who choose to postpone sexual intimacy until marriage often criticized?

3. Do you believe that "fleeing" is the key when it comes to abstaining, and that the motivation to heed God's direction must outweigh the desire for sex? If so, what are some precautions that you can begin taking today?

4. When it comes to finding the right person, do you agree that God will reward you as you honor Him? Do you agree that it's best to avoid dating just for the sake of dating? Why? Why not?

5. Can you see the person that you are dating or courting as the life-long mother, or father, of your children? Will they be someone you can respect years down the road? Will they be someone who remains committed to the marriage and to God even through difficult times? If not, it may be wise to reconsider the relationship.

Recommended Reading:
Choosing God's Best by Dr. Don Rannikar
The Book of Romance by Tommy Nelson

For those desiring more information on the subject of sex, dating, and marriage, check out *Focus on the Family* at www.family.org.

Unfortunately, we remember our past mistakes far more than God's faithfulness, and our heartbreaks more than His healing power.

———————

The walls we build to protect may eventually imprison.

CHAPTER SIX

BROKEN
Yet Unbreakable

The one who will never leave

L IFE IS A LONG JOURNEY FULL OF WONDERFUL opportunities and experiences, but there are also roadblocks, delays, pitfalls, and hurdles. We overcome by persevering; by getting up when we fall. Successful people build success from failure. They don't look back—it's not the direction they want to go. Everyone falls, but not everyone gets up. Few things hinder us more than failing to forgive others or ourselves for past mistakes. Many times, they haunt and discourage us from moving forward. As a result, people may rate themselves according to who they were, or what they did; not realizing that who they are now, and who they will become is far more important.

With life comes power. The God-given power to persevere is one of the strongest attributes that we possess. **The obstacles ahead are never greater than God's power**

to take you through. There is little that we can do about life's difficulties, except control the way that we respond to them. *It's been said that life is 10 percent what happens to us and 90 percent how we react to it.* We are clearly in charge of our attitudes and responses.

Granted, I don't have all of the answers, and there are questions and situations that are difficult to understand, but II Corinthians 4:8-9 has helped me greatly, and it can help you too. It states: "We are hard-pressed on every side, yet not crushed; we are perplexed, but not in despair; persecuted, but not forsaken; struck down, but not destroyed." When I was hard-pressed, I was molded into the person that He intended me to be. When I was perplexed, I had only to ask for direction and move forward. When I was persecuted, I found hope through spiritual truths. When I was struck down, God restored me, and when I wanted to give up, I found the endless encouragement to continue. God will do the same for you as you commit your life to Him. **You will find encouragement, restoration, and wholeness in the One who will never leave nor forsake you.**

The last thing you ever want to do

With millions of families experiencing divorce, abuse, or broken relationships, the need to address this topic is unavoidable and necessary. In the book, *Sacred Thirst*, the author writes:

> The bride and groom are standing in front of everyone, looking better than they are ever going to look again, getting so much attention and affirmation. Everybody even stands when they walk in, so it's easy to think this marriage, at least, is about them. It's not. Just look at the worn-out

parents sitting in the first pew—they understand this. The only reason these parents are still married is because long ago they learned how to handle the hurt they caused each other. **They know that the last thing you ever want to do with hurt is to let it define you.**[31]

 ... those who do not allow hurt to entrap them can turn brokenness into an unbreakable force, but those shackled by past pain are truly imprisoned by it.

The last sentence is powerful: those who do not allow hurt to entrap them can turn brokenness into an unbreakable force, but those shackled by past pain are truly imprisoned by it. The walls we build to protect may eventually imprison. Whether you are a teenager whose parents have divorced, or a young adult living with the pain of a broken home, abuse, neglect, or abandonment, **God can rebuild your brokenness into an unbreakable force.**

Years ago, I heard an interview with a survivor of the Holocaust. She described the horrific conditions of the concentration camps, and then she made a statement that I'll never forget. She described the emotional pain and the brokenness she experienced from her divorce as greater than the pain of the concentration camp. Unbelievable! A person who experienced more pain than most of us will ever know said that a broken relationship was more painful than the fear of being killed.

If you enter the marriage with the common attitude: "I'll try it out and see if it works," it probably won't.

In the case of marriage, the spiritual union of two people was never designed to be broken. We may try to hide the pain that lingers from a broken relationship, but it's there waiting for the opportunity to arise and consume us. Unless God rebuilds the foundation, those who have experienced severe pain and heartache never fully recover. The good news, however, is that the woman speaking on the radio recognized God's healing power. Regardless of what she had endured, God delivered her from the emotional scars. He can deliver those broken by abuse, abandonment, failed relationships, and broken homes as well, but change must first occur on the inside. Strongholds such as unforgiveness, bitterness, self-pity, pride, and anger hinder the healing and rebuilding process. Healing begins with a commitment to work on those areas—to let it go.

Couples today often want the freedom to divorce and leave the marriage if it doesn't work out. Keep this in mind as you move toward marriage: **marriage never works out; you have to work it out.** You may wonder why I'm talking to you about divorce and brokenness? First, many of you reading this have experienced the pain that a divorce brings to the family. Second, **your perception of marriage before you marry is crucial to the success of the relationship after you marry.** If you enter the marriage with the common attitude: "I'll try it out and see if it works," it probably won't. The health of your marriage must be a priority in your life even if you are not yet married. Although your parents may have divorced, it doesn't have to be an option for you. Your goal should be to form a lasting covenant with your spouse. That's why it's so important to choose the right person. *You won't find the perfect person, but with God's help, you will find the perfect person for you.*

How can you undo the emotional pain experienced from brokenness? First, God heals us with the transforming power of His word: "He sent His word and healed them, and delivered them from their destructions" (Psalm 107:20). My intent is not to disregard the emotional pain of brokenness, I've experienced it myself, but to remind you that God makes provision for our needs. He is the Great Physician; look to His Word for comfort and strength.

Second, of all the books that I've read, sermons that I've heard, people that I've talked with, and devastation that I've seen firsthand, one common denominator was present: *those who do not forgive or release bitterness and anger, never truly experience freedom, happiness, or true restoration.* Forgiveness is the key to healing. That's why it's often difficult to forgive someone who has wronged us. The enemy knows that forgiveness brings emotional health and spiritual wholeness, and he does what he can to keep us from it. Ephesians 4:31-32 states, "Let all bitterness, wrath, anger, clamor, and evil speaking be put away from you ... and be kind to one another, tenderhearted, forgiving one another, even as God in Christ forgave you." If we fail to forgive others, bitterness and anger can and will prevent emotional restoration. No matter what your situation is, God can turn brokenness into an unbreakable force; but it is important that your mind is first renewed, beginning with forgiveness, and repentance, if warranted. **Pain can make us bitter, or it can make us better—ultimately, it's our choice.** *God restores if we are willing to forgive.*

If Christ died for us and forgave us, surely we can forgive those who have wronged us. In certain circumstances, however, this can be extremely difficult. Although forgiveness is a decision, building trust is a process. Forgiving someone doesn't mean that we instantly trust them again or continue the relationship. In some cases, it's wise to keep our distance, especially in cases of abuse where danger or serious harm is involved.

Although we cannot control the choices others make, we can control the way that we respond to them. For example, if your parents have chosen to separate or divorce, you may attempt to influence or encourage them to remain together, but ultimately the choice to leave or to stay is up to them. God has given us the freedom to choose, and, in marriage, the choices of one can greatly affect the life of the entire family. But God can honor and bless your circumstance if you trust Him and forgive others. He can rebuild your life and open doors you might not have thought possible. Meanwhile, continue to pray and contend for the restoration of your family.

Above all else

Proverbs 4:23 (NLT) says, "Above all else, guard your heart, for it affects everything you do." Few things can hinder our lives more than misguided emotions. When we're down and have a negative attitude, it's difficult to find the motivation to see things through. Our enemy does not want a well-guarded heart; he wants us exposed and vulnerable.

He wants us so emotionally scarred from past relationships that we spend years trying to rebuild our lives. Guarding our heart should be a priority, not a consideration. **Guarding your heart means guarding your mind.** It's been said that one of the most damaging emotions is misplaced anger. After all, he who angers you controls you; he or she controls you indirectly through your consuming thoughts. When the apostle Paul wrote, "Let all bitterness, wrath, anger, clamor, and evil speaking be put away from you," he understood that in order for a Christian to be effective, anger should find no place to dwell. Proverbs 14:17 states, "A quick-tempered man acts foolishly." Don't react; instead respond, and sometimes it's best not to respond at all. As Abraham Lincoln once suggested, "Better to remain silent and be thought a fool than to speak out and remove all doubt." Think before you act. A reaction often calls for an apology, while a response generally thinks things through and, often, no apologies are needed. This can be hard at times, especially when your home resembles a volcano on the verge of erupting.

Anger is not necessarily wrong. Ephesians 4:26-27 says, "Be angry, and do not sin: do not let the sun go down on your wrath, nor give place to the devil." Anger over issues that anger the Lord, such as abortion, abuse, oppression, pornography, and so on, is justifiable and can cause positive

❝❝ *Better to remain silent and be thought a fool than to speak out and remove all doubt.* **❞❞**

—ABRAHAM LINCOLN

Anger cannot be harnessed on its own. Only the transforming Word of God and a personal relationship with Christ, along with the work of the Holy Spirit, brings life-long healing.

action. If anger causes damage to another, or personally damages your character, it's probably not accomplishing God's purpose; your emotional health will be affected. If anger sparks prayer and a Christ-like stance, it's productive. This may have been why Martin Luther said, "When I am angry, I can pray well and preach well."

James 1:20 says, "For the wrath of man does not produce the righteousness of God." **We'll rarely settle an argument, or win a dispute, with anger.** We are encouraged to weigh our actions carefully and respond accordingly. Granted, this is easier said than done, but it can be done as we seek to be "filled" with the Holy Spirit. We have responsibilities, but spiritual growth is His department; don't become frustrated.

If anger is not dealt with while a person is single, it will enter into the marriage; this is especially true with men. As a result, wives can become targets of the anger, and the marriage will suffer. Don't take this issue lightly; anger is very destructive. If you're a female currently dating a man who becomes easily angered, I strongly suggest that you reconsider the relationship; or, that he learns to control his anger before a serious commitment is even considered. This can take time. For many years, I had a difficult time controlling my temper, and, at times, it's still a challenge. Anger cannot be harnessed on its own. Only the transforming Word of God and a personal relationship with Christ, along with the work of the Holy Spirit, brings life-long healing. It sounds redundant, but it's true: *a daily relationship with Christ along with prayer and Scripture reading can eventually calm an angry spirit.* Recall Romans 8:6 (NLT): "If your sinful nature controls your mind, there is death. But if the Holy Spirit controls your mind, there is life and peace." With God's help, you'll begin to control anger instead of allowing anger to control you.

A choice, not a feeling

If the most dangerous emotion is misplaced anger, then it is safe to assume that the Bible's definition of love is the best way to guard the heart and restore emotional health. The Bible defines love this way (try replacing the word "love" with your name): "Love is patient, love is kind. It does not envy, it does not boast, it is not proud. It is not rude, it is not self-seeking, it is not easily angered, it keeps no record of wrongs. Love does not delight in evil but rejoices with the truth. It always protects, always trusts, always hopes, always perseveres" (I Corinthians 13:4-7 NIV). This is how we are to love our parents, our friends, our brothers, our sisters, and so on; even our enemies. Love doesn't say, "That's your problem, deal with"; it says, "How can I help you?" **True love is a choice, not a feeling.** *If love is the greatest commandment, it should be our first priority.* When our concept of love is different than God's, we get into trouble, and our emotions suffer.

Love hopes for and believes the best in others; it's demonstrated through your actions and your words. You may not always see the best in others, but you should trust that it's there, and encourage it to grow. Strive to develop the type of love that protects and defends others. For instance, catch yourself when you're tempted to gossip or belittle others; or turn the direction of the conversation if someone is taking you in that direction. The Bible is clear: *if you have not love, it profits you nothing.* You can be well read in all sixty-six books of the Bible, preach as well as Billy Graham, and have a Ph.D. in theology, but if you don't have love, you have nothing. (Refer to I Corinthians 13:1-3.) **Make love and forgiveness your top priority; they will not rise to that level left alone.**

Remember that relationships are like checking accounts. *Words of healing and praise are deposits into our emotional bank account; words of anger and insults are withdrawals.* If there are more withdrawals than deposits, the account not only loses value, but it can create emotional bankruptcy. Emotional bankruptcy happens frequently in relationships, especially in the family. "Death and life are in the power of the tongue" (Proverbs 18:21). Negative words and/or a lack of positive words can play an enormous role in our emotional health—even the words we say about ourselves. Choose your words carefully and encourage, not discourage, the success of others.

The Bible directs us to *be slow to speak* (James 1:19). We're human, and from time to time we say and do things that hurt others; others say and do things that hurt us. God instructs us to overlook the wrongs done against us, and, hopefully, others will do the same. Keep the emotional bank account open. I'm not suggesting that you allow chronic physical, emotional, or verbal abuse—seek help from those who will give scriptural counsel, and never underestimate the power of prayer.

If you're not sure if a person is a positive influence in your life, consider where they are leading you; is it in the direction that you want to go?

Friend or foe—what you need to know

Not only will unforgiveness and anger affect emotional health, people will too. **People either lift you up, or pull you down.** As stated earlier: if you are standing on a wall, it's easier to be pulled down than to pull someone up. Likewise, the downward pull of a destructive relationship is strong. Proverbs 18:24 says that *there are friends who destroy each other,* and II Corinthians 6:14 states, "Do not be unequally yoked together with unbelievers. For what fellowship has righteousness with lawlessness? And what communion has light with darkness?" Although this command is crystal clear, it's often read with clouded vision, especially as it relates to marriage. Companions, good or bad, influence our character.

Countless times in the Old Testament, God warned His people not to have friends who would draw them away from Him, and countless times their disregard led to their downfall. **Who we associate with may be who we become.** If you're not sure if a person is a positive influence in your life, consider where they are leading you; is it in the direction that you want to go? If not, seriously reconsider the relationship. I cannot stress this enough. Of all the negative relationships that I have ended over the years, I have not regretted ending any. It's easy to believe that you'll influence the other person by lifting them up, but often, they have the stronger leverage to pull you down. Destructive relationships do exactly that— pull you down.

If a "friend" does not have the qualities that you're looking for, don't lower your standards, keep them high. **Many times, the problem isn't that we raise our standard and miss it, it's that we lower it and hit it.** Please understand that I am not suggesting that Christians only interact with other Christians; we are called to minister to others in all areas of life. We cannot totally separate from the culture. What good is salt if it's left in the shaker? But if the friendship is pulling you in the wrong direction, it's time to re-evaluate the relationship. Hebrews 12:1 tells us to remove every weight and burden that slows us down. Negative relationships are both. (Check out II Timothy 3:1-5.)

Build success from failure

As you begin to rebuild and restore your life, expect opposition. The enemy will oppose you through self-doubt, guilt, anger, unforgiveness, etc. He'll use pessimistic people and/or fill your mind with negative thoughts in an attempt to discourage you. Those trying to rebuild a marriage may be taunted by the thought, "It's useless; why try?" Those trying to rebuild a broken past may think, "I've done too much damage. God can't use me now." The enemy emphasizes the negative, but God, not the enemy, oversees the rebuilding process. *When God is for you, no one can stand against you. God is greater than the problem that you are facing.* The key is to focus on what He can and will do in your life even though no evidence is seen. Hebrews 11:1 reminds us that "faith is the substance of things hoped for, the evidence of things not seen." Faith believes God's promises before they happen. Simply stated, stay focused on the goal of emotional restoration, not on the opposition.

Most of us feel depressed from time to time as a result of our human condition. Physical conditions, unfavorable circumstances, chemical imbalances, spiritual attacks, or combinations of these can create feelings of sadness, despair, dependency, and hopelessness. How do you avoid the emotional roller coaster? First, check the obvious and make the needed adjustments:

- Who are you associating with? What are you watching or listening to? Is it building you up, or pulling you down?

- Do you allow negative thoughts to gain a stronghold? Are you spending time praying each day?

- Are you walking in obedience to God's Word?

- Are you living under God's grace, or under the constraints of legalism?

- Are you measuring success according to God's standard, or the world's?

- Are there past pains or unresolved issues that you haven't dealt with?

- Do you harbor unforgiveness, bitterness, or anger?

- Are you taking care of your body? Are you making healthy food choices? Are you getting enough sleep?

- In short, are you building your relationship with Christ? Remember ... He is the Great Physician.

If you are doing all that you know to do and nothing seems to help, remember that the battle is the Lord's. We have responsibilities, yet we are totally dependent on God. We must do our part, but we can't do His. Mild depression and sadness are common to all of us, but when it lingers, it often requires more focused attention. Exercise, prayer, fun, friendship, forgiveness, and kindness actually fight against depression. Granted, there may be clear cases of depression that may require professional, biblically-based counseling. God may direct you to seek professional advice, or it may be a time of testing. Count on Him to see you through.

Don't overlook this area

In concluding this chapter on emotional health, we cannot ignore the importance of our *physical* health. Although we've discussed the health of our spirit and soul, little has been said about our physical health; therefore, it's time to shift gears.

The physical health of our body can definitely play a role in our overall health—mentally, emotionally, and spiritually. It's ironic ... we have more fitness centers, more personal trainers, more books, and more articles written about fitness than ever before, yet health-related illnesses and problems caused from poor nutrition and obesity are increasing at an alarming rate.

Society's view of nutrition often runs contrary to principles that promote "good health." For instance, as I was sitting in a popular café, a group of teenagers walked in before school and ordered extra large, chocolate coffee drinks topped with caramel and whipped-cream. No wonder many experience extremely low energy levels, attention-deficit problems, sleep disorders, anxiety, and mood swings, to name only a few. *Regardless of what the culture promotes, choosing to follow a healthier lifestyle is the first step in making health a priority.*

Health-related illnesses caused by poor nutrition are killing more Americans than anything else. Eating healthy is a constant challenge because temptation is always before us. The next time that you're tempted to eat something unhealthy, try asking, "Does my body need it—or does it want it?" If it needs it, consume it. If it wants it, think twice. **It's generally not "if" poor nutrition causes damage, but "when."** What a sad commentary on the lifestyle of a nation that has such great potential to live in the blessings that God has so graciously given.

The purpose of food is to meet our nutritional needs, not our wants. That bears repeating: food was created to meet our body's "needs" not our "wants." Many of America's most popular foods have little nutritional value, and contain harmful ingredients.[32] Add to this the absence of fruit and vegetables for fiber and dietary value, and it's obvious why cancer now affects one out of three individuals—we're not feeding the body what it needs to fight cancer, heart disease, and poor health, in general.

I encourage you to read food labels, and to know what you're consuming; trust me, you will be shocked. Many of the additives found in food today are simply there to enhance flavor, color, and appearance, and to substantially increase the shelf life of the product. Unfortunately, this approach is far from healthy. **We were created to consume living, life-sustaining, God-given foods that nourish and support a healthy body, not dead, life-depleting food from a factory**. If you can avoid empty foods and consume more whole, life-giving foods, and limit caffeine consumption, you'll be well on your way to better health.

Many people spend most of their lives trying to look different. They often rate their appearance by society's

A perfect physique does not guarantee happiness anymore than a good mattress guarantees sleep.

standard and strive to look like a "perfect ten." This false perception causes many people to remain unfulfilled, even the "tens." When we compare ourselves to others, we are not using wisdom. You were not designed to be someone else; you were masterfully designed to be you. A perfect physique does not guarantee happiness anymore than a good mattress guarantees sleep. **True happiness does not come from outer appearance; it comes from spiritual health.**

Questions to consider for Chapter Six:

1. Do you agree that those who do not allow hurt to define them can turn brokenness into an unbreakable force, but those shackled by past pain are truly imprisoned by it? How can the prison doors be opened?

2. Do you agree that strongholds such as unforgiveness, bitterness, pride, and anger hinder the healing and rebuilding process? Are there any areas in your life that need to be dealt with before emotional and spiritual health can be fully restored?

3. After reading I Corinthians 13:4-7 again, highlight areas that need improvement: "Love is patient, love is kind. It does not envy, it does not boast, it is not proud. It is not rude, it is not self-seeking … ."

4. If relationships are like checking accounts, how can

you make more deposits than withdrawals even though others may not do the same?

5. Do you agree that it's not *if* poor nutrition causes damage, but *when*? If so, how can you begin making health a priority? What exact changes can be made?

Recommended Reading:
I Really Want to Change ... So, Help Me God
  by James MacDonald
When the Enemy Strikes by Charles Stanley

Recommended Reading for Health and Wellness:
Maximum Energy by Ted Broer
Toxic Relief by Don Colbert
The Makers Diet by Jordan Rubin

I also wrote a book based on my own experience: *What Works When "Diets" Don't.*

The lectures you deliver may be very wise and true; but I'd rather get my lesson by observing what you do. For I may misunderstand you and the high advice you give, but there's no misunderstanding how you act and how you live.

—Edgar A. Guest

———————

Reputation is who you are around others. Character is who you are when others aren't around.

CHAPTER SEVEN

What's INSIDE?

What's inside spills out

AS A CHILD, I was captured by the stories that my grandfather told about life on the farm in Oklahoma in the early 1900s. The images I've held are not those of pleasant surroundings and ideal conditions; they are impressions of twelve-hour days spent working the land, dust storms that could devastate a crop, blistered and sunburned skin, and poverty unlike most Americans know today. Life, in general, was harder then, but interestingly enough, character seemed much stronger—it was a time when commitment, integrity, and honesty stood in place of contracts, disclosures, and bylaws. A handshake and a man's word were generally good enough. I'm not suggesting that we return to that time in history, but that we learn from the past and strongly encourage those same character traits today.

... the depth of your relationship with God is in direct proportion to the depth of your commitment to Him; great commitment, great relationship; poor commitment, poor relationship. Discipline matters!

I remember watching a news story about an enormous oil tanker that sprung a leak off the coast of Spain. Because the tanker was full of oil, millions of gallons gushed into the sea; it was a horrific sight and an environmental disaster. In the same way, **when we're struck, what's inside spills out.** Is anger, pride, unforgiveness, or selfishness exposed, or does adversity reveal patience, humility, forgiveness, and self-control?

Much of what we've discussed, thus far, focuses largely on developing spiritual disciplines and godly character (what's on the inside). Discipline is the ability to put the right choice into action; it's essential for accomplishing anything in this life. If we exercise discipline in one area, it will help to strengthen other areas. Habits are hard to break, and it often takes discipline to overcome them. The principle of discipline cannot be overlooked when it comes to developing godly character.

Ironically, **people think that they lack discipline, but they don't—they lack motivation.** For instance, if it were possible to offer a large sum of money to those who would read their Bible an hour a day for six months, how many would qualify for the money? Probably a large percentage would. The motivation of receiving money would outweigh the lack of desire to read the Bible. Isn't spiritual health far more valuable than money? But the excuse that I hear most often is: "I don't have enough time!" How often have we said or heard others say that they don't have enough time in their day? I want to challenge those, who, like myself, do have time to put first things first. We often forget just how precious time is. How many weeks, months, or even years do we waste because we don't prioritize our lives? We need to be very careful when we say that we don't have enough time, because what we are sometimes saying is that it's not important enough.

We claim that we don't have time for God, but we find plenty of time to play sports, watch television, pursue hobbies, or go out with friends. I've fallen into this trap myself, and I've noticed that the real issue isn't time, but rather how I choose to spend it. If we don't schedule time, time will schedule for us. *Time is not like money; it can't be earned, borrowed, or saved. You do, however, spend it, so spend wisely.* Ask, "What's the most important thing for me to do in any given hour?" Contrary to what many think, reading the Bible and praying actually help with the utilization of time; they instill into our lives: discipline, commitment, patience, peace, joy, and contentment. I've also found that it seems that my time, like money, is multiplied when I give first to God. If we're too busy to place God first—we're too busy! I like what pastor John

If we're too busy to place God first—we're too busy!

MacArthur said about studying God's Word: "I use a system I call 'planned neglect': I plan to neglect everything else until my studying is done."[33] As a matter of fact, the depth of your relationship with God is in direct proportion to the depth of your commitment to Him; great commitment, great relationship; poor commitment, poor relationship. Discipline matters!

All this talk about discipline and character can seem overwhelming. The key is to take small steps and focus on the goal of character development rather than on the process of change. Don't tackle these issues on your own; rely on God's strength to see you through.

Are you working hard toward your goals, and are you working smart? It's never too late. The ability to "stick to it" is what separates those who succeed from those who almost succeed. You've been given the power to make decisions, the power to develop character, and the power to choose at any given time. Many are willing to break a habit, get good grades, follow through on commitments, lose weight, save money, attend church, seek God more fervently, and so on, but willingness alone is not enough. Willingness must be followed by action, and action, in this sense, is simply discipline in motion.

The only way to build into our lives such qualities as love, joy, peace, humility, and patience is to be confronted with situations that require love, joy, peace, humility, and patience.

Trying times

Ponder this question ... "Why is character development and keeping our word so challenging?" Is it because we do not want to change? Is it because we cannot change? Or, is it because we don't know how to change? The answer is simple, in a sense. In general, our culture isn't concerned with "what's inside"; it often does not encourage the development of integrity, commitment, or godly character. If we're not careful, things such as jealousy, pride, laziness, envy, gossip, bitterness, and dishonesty will begin to dominate our decisions and ultimately tarnish our character. Building godly character is challenging because it's constantly under attack. How many movies and television programs encourage positive character traits? Not many.

Developing godly character requires that we are tested, trained, and disciplined, but the rewards far outweigh the pain. **Trying times are not intended to break us down, but, ultimately, to build us up.** Imagine a man entering the Marines. He knows that he wants to be a Marine, but he has no idea what to expect. The first day he is awe-struck by what's required of him, but the countless hours of training, the ongoing testing, and the discipline to remain committed eventually pay off. He graduates a Marine. Was the process easy? Hardly! It was the most difficult training that he'd ever faced. A soldier doesn't attend boot camp for a few hours, take a test, and simply go home. The process of becoming a Marine is rigorous and intense. Likewise, when God develops character, He does so to meet the challenges ahead, to prepare us for life, and to mold us into Christ's image. The only way to build into our lives such qualities as love, joy, peace, humility, and patience is to be confronted with situations that require love, joy, peace, humility, and patience. How do we develop patience if we're not tested? How do we develop forgiveness if we are never wronged? How do we learn to trust God if we're never in need? How do we develop character if we are never challenged? James 1:2-4 actually advises us to "count it all joy when you fall into various trials, knowing that the testing of your faith produces patience. But let patience have its perfect work, that you may be perfect and complete, lacking nothing." **"The Lord gets His best soldiers out of the highlands of affliction"** (Charles Spurgeon).

Collapse is certain

As you develop godly character, pay close attention to the deception of *pride*. Pride is the opposite of humility, and its collapse is certain. Pride can be defined as conceit, or a sense of superiority in who we are, what we do, or in what we possess. The Lord hates pride, arrogance, and self-centeredness. When we think more highly of ourselves than we should, pride is a problem, and it will hinder character and spiritual development. Without humility and a teachable spirit, it's difficult, if not impossible, to defeat pride. *Humility does not mean that we become passive observers, but that we live in total surrender to God.*

In the Old Testament, for example, God gave people the opportunity to be leaders, but it was their character and their humility, not their position, that determined their outcome. That bears repeating: it's your character—"what's inside"—not your title or position in life, that matters. America has some of the most talented athletes, entertainers, and entrepreneurs in the world. Many rise to the top because of their ability, but

... husbands and wives don't marry one another filled with love and passion one day only to lose it the next. Marriage deteriorates because more attention is given to self than spouse.

plummet to the bottom because they lack godly character. Reputation is who you are around others; character is who you are when others aren't around.

There is another aspect of pride that we dare not ignore, especially in the Christian community: *spiritual pride.* Spiritual pride often goes unnoticed; it's a silent sin. For example, some who have refrained from sex until marriage or who have grown spiritually more than others, may have the tendency to think of themselves as better. They view themselves as the "spiritually mature," positioned above everyone else. Spiritual pride is also present when we think that our Christian denomination is the "only" right one. Although challenging at times, it's much easier to walk in humility than it is to stumble through life selfishly with the prospect of being humbled by the Lord. Humility is an attitude that God blesses.

If our eyes are continually fixed on the faults of others, an entire lifetime can be wasted because of pride. God does mighty things in the lives of those who are teachable and humble. Proverbs 18:12 (NIV) states it well: "Before his downfall a man's heart is proud, but humility comes before honor." Be careful: the higher up you think you are, the farther you can fall.

❝ *... the eyes of the Lord run to and fro throughout the whole earth to show Himself strong on behalf of those whose hearts are loyal to Him.* **❞**

(II Chronicles 16:9)

God intended that we love people and use things; instead, we tend to love things and use people. Pride causes us to take pleasure in the things of the world, rather than in the things of God. As you move toward marriage, consider this: husbands and wives don't marry one another filled with love and passion one day only to lose it the next. Marriage deteriorates because more attention is given to self than spouse. Most who are divorced will say that their marriage was initially good, but, with time, one or both stopped loving—largely because of selfishness. Develop humility and godly character now so they can strengthen your marriage in the future. But keep in mind that these things are accomplished through the power of the Holy Spirit operating in a believer's life. Trying to do these things in our own strength can bring frustration and failure.

What else can be done to further develop character? First, commit the battle to Christ. Second, keep your word and follow through on your commitments: "A man is only as good as his word." Third, let integrity be your guiding light. Fourth, **remember that the enemy *goes about like a roaring lion seeking whom he may devour*** (I Peter 5:8). But be encouraged, *the eyes of the Lord also run to and fro throughout the whole earth to show Himself strong on behalf of those whose hearts are loyal to Him* (II

Chronicles 16:9). The question is, "Who finds you?" Are you loyal to God by obeying His Word, or do you stray from the Shepherd and become easy prey?

It takes time to develop godly character; don't get discouraged. Although character is a matter of choice, it's also forged through affliction and tempered by adversity; it's built through the challenges that we face and the obstacles that we overcome. Our character provides the material on which we build our lives and our relationships. Many spend years trying to rebuild their life simply because their foundation is weak. Make no mistake about it: *a strong foundation will cost you something, but a weak foundation may cost you everything.* The foundation that you build today provides the strength that weathers the storm tomorrow. How strong is your foundation?

To young men

Sometime ago, my mother gave me a faded note in the form of a prayer that she wrote for her children years ago. She listed several character traits that men should strive to possess.

Seek to be a man who

... sincerely desires to love and serve the Lord.

... hungers for a righteous spirit, and is honest at all times, despite the cost.

 A strong foundation will cost you something, but a weak foundation may cost you everything.

... chooses words and actions that are wise and well thought through, considering first the consequences.

... desires to protect, preserve, and appreciate the beauty in a woman, and recognizes his strength and masculinity as created by God.

... focuses on the needs of others rather than on his own, and is not critical and domineering when communicating.

... works hard, and will stop at nothing to accomplish what God has set before him.

... stretches the limits of his body, soul, and spirit to excel in every area possible.

... desires to encourage and nurture others, rather than to overpower and control.

... seeks excellence in all things and lives to that end.

For young women

I asked my wife if she could close this chapter on character by briefly commenting on an issue that many young women face today.

Morgan writes ...

Any guess as to what my topic might be? It's modesty, or the lack of it in today's culture. I know that this topic may tempt you to skip this section entirely, but bear with me; it's something that we definitely need to discuss.

We must understand that how we dress affects the thoughts of the men that we come in contact with. Although many women like attention, our motivation to develop godly character should outweigh our need

What women view as "fashion" is often a major temptation for men.

for attention; we have certain responsibilities before God.

As fun as it is to shop, I must admit that I've been very frustrated with the latest fashion trends—shorts that look like they would fit a five-year-old, and shirts that reveal more than they cover. Whatever happened to modesty? For some reason, we feel that we must dress seductively to be popular. After all, everyone is doing it.

Dressing modestly is challenging because we have been conditioned by what society considers attractive: short, tight, and revealing. Instead, **try not to view clothing as fashion, but as a statement that tells people who you are and what you stand for** (this can apply to men as well). This isn't to say that we should only wear oversized or unfashionable clothing; we should care about our appearance, but if our clothing becomes a stumbling block for guys, an adjustment definitely needs to be made. The enemy tempts guys with lust, and we often become distractions for them. This fact alone should cause us to reconsider our attire. Granted, fashion and modesty are sometimes a challenge for me, even now. As a matter of fact, it was difficult when I finally decided to go through my closet and weed out the inappropriate clothes, but the more I focused on doing the right thing and less on gaining attention, the transition became easy.

Don't become frustrated; change takes time. After I became a Christian, God really had to deal with my heart on this issue. I had excuses like: "If he can't control his desires, that's his problem," or, "Everyone is wearing this—what's the big deal?" But that wasn't the right attitude. What women view as "fashion" is often a major temptation for men. Men are stimulated visually. Although the responsibility for their thoughts does not rest solely on us, we should do our part to lessen their temptation. Here are a few things that we can do based on some of the principles that Shane covered earlier:

First, a personal relationship with Jesus Christ is so important—it's through this relationship, and only through this relationship, that you will be able to put things in the right perspective and make the right choices.

Second, I encourage you to look to God's Word, not the media, for direction and encouragement. Many times, we don't make the right choices because we are influenced by the fashion industry rather than by God's standard.

Third, choose the pain of discipline over the pain of regret. This is a tough one. Why do we cringe at the sound of discipline? Probably because we associate it with doing something difficult, when in reality, discipline simply means putting into action the right choice. I have learned that the joys of choosing discipline far outweigh the consequences that come with lasting regret.

Fourth, be prepared for society's influence, and do what you can to keep a positive outlook—a godly outlook. Prior to meeting Shane, I struggled daily with jealousy, and still struggle at times. Inevitably, my thoughts began to hinder our relationship. *Some of my struggle was linked to the fashion world's perception of what a woman should look like, not God's.* When we follow God's plan for our lives, we value His opinion more than society's. Focus on doing what is right, regardless of what today's culture promotes—it's worth it!

Fifth, I found that the most important role is not that of a model or actress, but of a woman who fears the Lord. Today's culture combines beauty and seduction as one, but God tells us otherwise. Be who the Lord wants you to be. This brings true satisfaction.

Sixth, look to God's Word for examples of character and integrity. Although a lot has been said about character, I'd like to share a closing thought. Although I trusted Christ as my Savior when I was 18, it took time to break certain patterns that had developed during my teen years. Looking back, I hardly recognize the girl that I once was. God has turned my past regrets into a future full of hope. Don't get discouraged, character is often built from the struggles that we face and the difficulties that we overcome. God's commandments

 Granted, it's often difficult to dress modestly in an immodest world, but it can be done as we examine our motives.

are designed to protect, not to prevent us from enjoying life. Granted, it's often difficult to dress modestly in an immodest world, but it can be done as we examine our motives. **Ask the Holy Spirit for guidance, and look to God for your sense of worth and value.** I encourage you to read Proverbs 31:10-31 often. You'll soon find that inner beauty is far more valuable than outward appearance. Remember that you were created for a purpose; your life has meaning. Regardless of how others have made you feel, God created you; you are not an accident. No matter what you've gone through or are going through, God's Word provides encouragement and direction as you face tough decisions—it's the solid rock on which our lives rest.

Questions to consider for Chapter Seven:

1. When you're struck with adversity, what spills out? Is anger, pride, unforgiveness, or selfishness exposed, or does adversity reveal patience, humility, forgiveness, and self-control? How can you better control what comes out?

2. Why is it so important to keep your word and follow through on commitments (even seemingly small commitments)? If this is an area that needs improvement, what changes can you begin making today? Do you agree that a man is only as good as his word? If so, explain.

3. How will you develop patience if you're not tested? How about forgiveness if you're never wronged? How will you develop character if you're never challenged? Are you being challenged this week?

4. If the foundation you build today provides the

strength that weathers the storm tomorrow, what are some of the ways that you can strengthen your foundation?

5. If you're a young man, what did you learn from the section to the young men? If you're a young woman, what did you learn from the section written specifically to young women?

Recommended Reading for Young Men:
The Quest for Character by John MacArthur
Disciplines of a Godly Man by R. Kent Hughes
The Man God Uses by Chuck Smith
Finishing Strong by Steve Farrar

Recommended Reading for Young Women:
Secret Keeper: The Delicate Power of Modesty
    by Dannah Gresh
Passion and Purity: Learning to bring your love life under Christ's control by Elisabeth Elliott

America is great because she is good, and if America ever ceases to be good, she will cease to be great.

—Commonly attributed to
Alexis De Tocqueville

———————

The only thing necessary for the triumph of evil is for good men [and women] to do nothing.

—Edmund Burke

ONE NATION
'Above' God

A note regarding Chapter Eight

As I complete this final chapter, war rages in the Middle East, and the potential for nuclear war intensifies. America is divided on many fronts. Where are the answers? How will the future and security of America unfold in the days to come?

Although the previous chapters address personal issues, the following chapter recognizes the biblical foundation that once guided America; these principles are the foundation on which America's success rests. This transition in subject matter may seem like a quantum leap, but stay with me.

Please understand that it is not my intention to endorse a political policy, party, or candidate—but to point, once again, to the power of Scripture to shape an individual, as well as a nation. Who we are in our personal lives should reflect who we are as a nation.

With that said, let's begin.

Keep the roots alive

NTERESTINGLY ENOUGH, one of the top concerns on the minds of young adults today is the stability of America. There was a time in recent history when America felt secure knowing that its most formidable enemies were abroad. Not so today. We seem to be losing ground in many areas. As a result, our legacy as a great nation has all but been forgotten.

"What does this have to do with young adults?" you might ask; it has everything to do with your future. Most schools are no longer teaching students about the spiritual foundation that has guided America throughout the years. Consequently, America's moral and religious heritage is often deleted, grossly distorted, or revised altogether. *Students often miss the critical connection between America's unparalleled greatness, her rise to world leadership, and the spiritual foundation that made it possible.* This should concern us. The ideas of the classroom in one generation will create the ideas of government within the next. **The spiritual state of a nation simply reflects the spiritual state of her people.** As things stand, the future of America will be an atmosphere of even greater intolerance of those committed to God's ways. If we fail to return to our Judeo-Christian roots, we will lose a rich harvest of God's blessings and experience the pain of regret.

In order to take the initial steps to regain lost ground, it's important to understand why America was established, and it's equally important to note just how far we have drifted from the original intent of the founding principles. Woodrow Wilson rightly said, "A nation which does not remember what it was yesterday, does not know what it is today, nor what it is trying to do."[34]

There are people and groups who are strongly committed to the destruction of anything rooted in our nation's Christian heritage. They want to be "One nation 'above' God," rather than "One nation 'under' God."

Although the history of America is marked with disappointments, tragedies, mistakes, and failures, my goal is not to write about the history of America, but to unapologetically proclaim the truth behind her success. Please take this chapter seriously. My intent is not to alarm you but to demonstrate the importance of regaining lost ground.

I'm a firm believer that if we don't water the roots, the plants will die. As a kid during the summer, one of my jobs was to water the flowerpots that lined our front and back patios. It was a simple job, but I was easily bored and anxious to finish. After quickly sprinkling the plants now and then for a few weeks, most of the flowers withered and died. Rather than a lecture, my mother felt that the best way to teach me responsibility and the need to soak the roots was to have me replace the flowers with my allowance. I learned a valuable lesson that summer: *keep the roots alive.* In the same way, if we fail to keep America's spiritual roots alive, the fruit of that blessing will wither and die.

There is a moral and cultural war raging in America and abroad. There are people and groups who are strongly committed to the destruction of anything rooted in our nation's Christian heritage. They want to be "One nation

> We, like the mighty Roman
> Empire that collapsed centuries
> ago, are crumbling from within.

'above' God," rather than "One nation 'under' God." While we're concerned with terrorist attacks, and rightly so, there is a greater threat from corruption within. We, like the mighty Roman Empire that collapsed centuries ago, are crumbling from within. There is a saying that *one generation plants trees for the next generation.* I'm concerned that instead of planting, we are removing and destroying the very covering that protects us.

Nearly 400 years ago, many sacrificed their lives and their families to promote Christian values. They set sail for a land where God's law would govern, and America was born. Many of America's Founding Fathers understood God's design for a prosperous life. They are found, not in the government, but in God alone, and it was on this foundation that America was built.

Today, our culture promotes *relativism,* and man does what is right in his own eyes. God's Word says to confront, confess, and turn from our sins; relativism encourages us to ignore, overlook, and continue in them. Abortion and illicit sex are now determined by personal preference rather than by God's Word. Pornography is commonly protected as an expression of free speech while school prayer is often banned. Our society clearly reflects man's digression from God. This detour cannot produce safe, secure living: "Woe to those who call evil good, and good evil" (Isaiah 5:20). Fortunately, God will continue to call from each generation those who will support His principles. I believe that many of you reading this are called to support these truths.

John Chalfant, a member of the Council for National Policy, said it best: "If we participate in dragging down our country by refusing to become involved when we are commanded to be virtuous and to let our convictions be known, do we deserve to be free?"[35] And Edmund Burke penned these words many years ago: "The only thing necessary for the triumph of evil is for good men [and women] to do nothing." **The price of freedom is not free. The moral state of our nation cannot be left to chance.**

Then vs. now— it's almost unbelievable

For those who doubt that America was founded on biblical principles, the following facts may surprise you. To understand the core values of a nation, one must simply look to the beliefs set forth during its conception. Judge for yourself how far we have drifted.

For starters, history reveals that if a proposed article for the Constitution was not supported by, or rooted in the Scriptures, it was not allowed in the Constitution. As a matter of fact, in their early writings, **many of the Founding Fathers quoted or referenced the Bible nearly four times more than any other source.**[36] Consider the following additional facts:

God's Word says to confront, confess, and turn from our sins; relativism encourages us to ignore, overlook, and continue in them.

Then: "That Book, Sir, is the rock on which our Republic rests." *President Jackson, although not a Founding Father, said this about the Bible as he lay on his deathbed.*[37]

Now: A U.S. District judge in Texas decreed that any student saying the name of Jesus at school graduation ceremonies would be jailed.[38] This is only one of many examples.

Then: *John Jay, the first Chief Justice of the U.S. Supreme Court,* said: "Unto Him who is the author and giver of all good, I render sincere and humble thanks for His manifold and unmerited blessings, and especially for our redemption and salvation by His beloved Son."[39]

Now: "It is unconstitutional for students to see the Ten Commandments since they might read, meditate upon, respect, or obey them."[40]

Then: *Noah Webster, the Founding Father of American Scholarship and Education,* said: "In my view, the Christian religion is the most important and one of the first things in which all children, under a free government, ought to be instructed ... ."[41] He believed so strongly in this that he often gave Scripture references when he defined words in his colossal work: *An American Dictionary of the English Language.* Sadly, his Scripture references have been withdrawn from recent editions.

Now: Many students are criticized when they read their Bibles at school, or in public. Christianity is mocked and ridiculed while just about every other belief is accepted and embraced.

Then: *The Delaware Constitution* initially required that "everyone appointed to public office must say, 'I do profess

❝❝ *It cannot be emphasized too strongly or too often that this great nation was founded, not by religionists, but by Christians; not on religions, but on the gospel of Jesus Christ.* **❞❞**

—Commonly Attributed to Patrick Henry

faith in God the Father, and in the Lord Jesus Christ his only Son ... .' "[42]

Now: Those who run for office and profess a faith in Jesus Christ are viewed as fanatical and/or extreme, and are often criticized by the media.

Then: *George Washington (America's first President) is credited with saying,* "**It is impossible to rightly govern the world without God and the Bible.**" Many statements like this from Washington prove that he was not a Deist, as some may suggest. (A Deist believes in an impersonal, distant God; they reject personal prayer as well as the Bible.)

Now: Bible displays and Ten Commandment monuments are ruled unconstitutional in courthouses and other public places.[43]

Very close to the edge

Unbelievable! And we've only touched the tip of the iceberg. It's amazing to see how far we have drifted. Clearly, most of America's Founders wanted the Bible and biblical principles so entrenched within society that nothing could remove them. This is why John Adams, one of the signers of the *Declaration of Independence*, rightly said: "The general principles on which the fathers achieved independence were ... the general principles of Christianity."[44]

The list could go on and on; from Harvard to Yale, from the Supreme Court to the local courts and the public school system, historically, the theme remained the same—God's Word was to be the foundation on which America was established! Even a brief review of the Founders *last wills and testaments* will confirm this. It's amazing to see how many of them acknowledged God and their Savior, Jesus Christ. Please understand that I'm not suggesting that the Founders were without flaws; they made many mistakes, but in general, they were committed to God's wisdom when they formed the government, and ultimately, the nation.

Patrick Henry, an American orator and statesman, and a leading patriot of the American Revolution, is credited with saying, "It cannot be emphasized too strongly or too often that this great nation was founded, not by religionists, but by Christians; not on religions, but on the gospel of Jesus Christ."[45] This is why 24 of the 56 signers of the *Declaration of Independence* were ministers of the gospel, and why the Supreme Court, in the early 1800s, ruled that public schools should teach the Bible.[46] This is why we cannot separate God's Word from governing our nation. This isn't a popular stance, or an easy one, but it's the right one! We need more people in leadership who recognize the need to return to our founding principles.

Unlike today, many early political leaders were not ashamed to admit the true source of America's strength— they were biblically correct, rather than politically correct. *They were statesmen, not politicians. A politician thinks of the next "election," a statesman of the next "generation."*

Can you imagine politicians acknowledging God and Jesus today; it would be unheard of. Granted, there are a few, and I thank them for their stance.

You may wonder, "Where is he going with this?" Straight to the point ... we're very close to the edge. Think of what this will mean to our children and grandchildren. If we fail to stand up for what is right—right now, we may see a time in our history when our freedoms, and their freedoms, will vanish. With the acceptance of gay-marriage and rejections to protect the unborn, that time is close at hand.

Psalm 11:3 states, "If the foundations are destroyed, what can the righteous do?" and the last half of Isaiah 7:9 (NIV) affirms, "If you do not stand firm in your faith, you will not stand at all." **This battle is for the very soul of our nation. It's our choice—do we stand or fall?**

A radical change that's changing America

With this much evidence supporting America's Christian heritage, why do so many deny it? Many criticize it because they acquire their information from "revisionists" or secular interpretations of what the Founders believed, rather than looking to the Founders' "original" writings. Others reject it because they reject God. Simply stated ... if there's a God (and there is), then the current direction of America's morality is wrong; something few want to admit.

There has been an ongoing, monumental debate in recent years about the government's role concerning religion. For those who understand the foundation on which the Constitution was built, there really is no debate. As a student, or young adult, you'll want to be aware of this misconception. Don't worry, this shouldn't bore you; I'll get straight to the point.

The State was to protect, administer justice, and defend the nation. The Church was to spread the gospel, guard the Word of God, and serve as the conscience of the people.

How have the courts been able to gradually remove God's Word from society? The misconception focuses primarily around the phrase "separation of Church and State." Although the First Amendment clearly says that *Congress shall not prevent religious expression*, the courts have ruled otherwise and have used the infamous "separation" phrase to ban religious activities, primarily those promoting Christian principles. Many believe that "separation of Church and State" appears in the Constitution, when in reality, the phrase does not appear anywhere in the Constitution. Did you catch that? "Separation of Church and State" does not appear in the Constitution. So where did it originate? Be very clear on this point, especially if you are a student in a public school or university, even a "Christian" university. Thomas Jefferson, author of the *Declaration of Independence*, used the phrase in a **private letter** written to the Baptist Association of Danbury, Connecticut.[47]

The Baptists feared that the government might someday try to regulate religious expression. (Remember, that's one reason why the Pilgrims left England.) In other words, they, like the Pilgrims, did not want the government imposing a national religion or denomination on the people—they wanted to worship freely. Mr. Jefferson wisely agreed with them, as did many of the other Founders. Jefferson assured them that Congress would neither establish a national denomination, nor prohibit the free exercise of religion, thus **protecting** religious expression by *building a wall of separation between the Church and the State*—solidifying the fact that the government could **not** strike down religious freedoms. If you doubt this, simply review the *Annals of Congress* from June 8th to September 25th, 1789.

Jefferson said that the freedom to express religion was a God-given right. However, approximately 150 years later, in 1947, the Supreme Court had other plans, and radically changed the meaning of the First Amendment. In *Everson v. Board of Education,* the Court said that the States could no longer engage in religious activities, and that the federal courts could now restrict such activities.[48] This is in complete opposition to what the Framers envisioned. **The Founding Fathers wanted the State and the Church to be separate in their duties and functions, but interwoven in their core beliefs and principles.** The State was to protect, administer justice, and defend the nation. The Church was to spread the gospel, guard the Word of God, and serve as the conscience of the people. You may want to commit those last few sentences to memory. With that understanding, there's really no debate.

Just how serious is this issue? In a newsletter entitled, *Truth & Tyranny,* Coral Ridge Ministries made this powerful statement: "Church-state separation is a lie, and it is deadly. It was this lie that led the Warren Court to ban prayer in public school in 1962. **That ruling set in motion the speediest and most spectacular decline of any civilization in history."**[49] Does this statement seem outlandish? If so, consider this: talking, chewing gum, and making noise were the top three public school problems in the early sixties. Now it's been estimated that rape, robbery, and assault lead the list, with murder close behind. You be the judge.

It's important to note that for 150 years before the 1947 decision, the States had their own powers and rights, and the federal government could not infringe on them. Religious expression, especially of the Christian faith, was commonplace. The courts now have taken it upon themselves to assume the role of a law-making body, rather than a protector of the Constitution. Therefore, we should pray for our leaders—executive, legislative, and judicial.

Without a shadow of a doubt, the intent of the Founders was not to remove God's Word from society, but to promote it. *They were concerned about government directing religion, rather than religion directing government.* They wanted God's principles to shape national policy. **The wall that was designed to protect America's freedoms has now imprisoned her.** We have, beyond a doubt, drifted off course.

Drowning—one step at a time

The First Amendment (freedom of speech) was never intended to lead to the distribution of pornographic material, crude dialogue in the media, and an array of other misapplications. Many of the early Justices participated in drafting the Constitution; one can simply review their rulings in the courtroom—rulings reflect convictions. For example, in *The People v. Ruggles* (1811), the defendant was tried in court for saying vulgar things about Jesus and His mother. The defendant's attorney believed that he had an open and shut case, and that his client would **not** be convicted based on "freedom of speech." The Judge, however,

❝ *Of the 22 civilizations that have appeared in history, 19 of them collapsed when they reached the moral state America is in today.* **❞**

—Arnold Toynbee

did not agree because he understood the true intent of the First Amendment. The defendant was convicted, fined, and sentenced to three months in jail. In Judge Kent's words: *"Nothing could be more offensive to the virtuous part of the community, or more injurious to the tender morals of the young, than to declare such profanity lawful."*[50] This statement would be laughed at today.

I often wonder what the Founding Fathers would have done differently had they foreseen the destruction of the institution of marriage between a man and a woman, and the aborting of over 40 million babies? What would they have changed had they foreseen the day when God's Word would be removed from nearly all areas of society? *Many of the men and women who died for our freedoms did not die for what we are becoming today.* Many gave their lives in order that we would be "One Nation Under God," not above God.

A Fifth Division graveyard sign in Iwo Jima, Japan, states it well: "When you go home, tell them for us and say, *'For your tomorrows we gave our today.'*" What a travesty when we fail to honor those who gave their lives for the freedoms that we now enjoy. In the words of Father O'Brien who served in World War II: "It is the soldier, not the reporter, who has given us the freedom of the press. It is the soldier, not the poet, who has given us the freedom of speech. It is the soldier, not the campus organizer, who gives us the freedom

> **❝** *We will have to repent in this generation not merely for the hateful words and actions of the bad people but for the appalling silence of the good people.* **❞❞**
>
> —**Martin Luther King, Jr.**

to demonstrate." O'Brien continues: *"It is the soldier who salutes the flag, who serves beneath the flag, and whose coffin is draped by the flag, who allows the protester to burn the flag."* **"A people that values its privileges above its principles soon loses both"** (Dwight D. Eisenhower).

Historically, we know that God judged those nations who continually tolerated sin; wrong choices had devastating consequences. Arnold Toynbee, who wrote the impressive twelve volume, *A Study of History*, said: "Of the 22 civilizations that have appeared in history, 19 of them collapsed when they reached the moral state America is in today."[51] Unfortunately, countless people today are confusing God's patience with His approval. C.S. Lewis said, "The safest road to hell is the gradual one—the gentle slope, soft underfoot, without sudden turnings, without milestones, without signposts."[52] *We're often too smart to take large, deliberate plunges, but we're easily enticed to take one step at a time.*

One year, with summer approaching, I stepped into my in-laws' pool. My immediate reaction to the piercing cold water was to step out, but to avoid their comments, I continued down the steps. I stopped when the water reached my knees. After a few minutes, I continued to move slowly down, stopping for brief periods until I was fully submerged.

Each step was shocking, but gradually, I became comfortable with the cold water—my body accepted what was initially shocking. In the same way, we've become comfortable with sin, and what once alarmed us now amuses us. We continue to hear: "Come on in, it's not that bad, everyone is doing it!" And we step right in. **America has been desensitized one generation at a time, one court decision at a time, one compromise at a time, and we are drowning in a cesspool of relativism.** It's critical to return to God's Word before we're fully submerged.

This chapter is intended as a wake-up call! We are experiencing the rapid deterioration of a nation right before our eyes. This is not the time to remain silent. For those who believe that we should remain passive and silent, I challenge you to read the writings of the Old Testament Prophets. They lamented, shed tears, and pleaded with the people and the leaders to turn from their sins and to turn back to God. Even Jesus cried for Jerusalem when He saw that her destruction was near. The same cry goes out today in America where we increase our wealth but decrease our values. We search the heavens for the answers, but turn from the One who created them. We call ourselves a Christian nation, but we often reject the biblical principles that made America great. Sadly, we call this progress.

We call ourselves a Christian nation, but we often reject the biblical principles that made America great. Sadly, we call this progress.

Martin Luther King, Jr. said, "We will have to repent in this generation not merely for the hateful words and actions of the bad people but for the appalling silence of the good people." I hold the same opinion today.

This is not the time for passivity but for change. We've heard these questions before, and we will hear them again: if not now, when? If not here, where? If not us, who? God told the prophet Ezekiel that *He looked for a man from among them who would build a wall and stand in the gap before Him on behalf of the land that He might not destroy it, but He found no one* (Ezekiel 22:30). This was true in Ezekiel's day, and it's true today. We are drowning one step at a time, but God is still looking for a few good men and women to stand up for what is right—right now. This is a difficult message, I know, but *when we fail to confront, we confirm.* When we fail to confront destructive ideas and philosophies, we are in essence confirming them. **We cannot change what we will not confront.**

When to become involved, if at all

One of the most controversial issues today is the question of mixing religion and politics. One group believes that the church should be used as a political platform, the other advocates passivity. I don't have all the answers, but I can share a few thoughts.

First and foremost, we cannot deny our primary responsibility—to encourage people to turn to Christ as their Lord and Savior; this is how America will "truly" change from the inside out. **The No. 1 problem in America is not a political problem; it's a spiritual problem called sin.** *The primary goal of the church is not to become a political movement, but a spiritual influence.* Politics won't

We're not just talking about adding millions of dollars to the deficit; we're talking about aborting millions of babies. We're not only talking about providing housing for the poor; we're talking about creating life simply to destroy it. This shift requires Christians to stay closely involved.

save America anymore than a dumbbell will save someone drowning in the ocean. However, we cannot ignore our God-given civic responsibility and the impact that politics has on our society. America's leaders play an enormous role in shaping the direction of the Country. Events such as the American Revolution, the abolition of slavery, and the civil rights movement, to mention only a few, happened because Christians took action. Leadership matters!

In the realm of government, we understand that there are two areas of responsibility for us to consider. One area is God's eternal kingdom; the other is the world's political system. We have a responsibility to both, but God's eternal kingdom must be our primary focus. Our political system, ordained by God, oversees the affairs of men. Remember: the State and the Church are to be separate in their duties and functions, but interwoven in their core beliefs and principles. The *institution* of government was created by God to govern man—to protect, administer justice, and defend the nations. Granted, many governments, including our own, often fall short. Nevertheless, it's important to recognize the significance of government and to respect its authority. (Check out Romans 13:1-7.)

Second, we should not overlook our civic duties as Christians. If 50 percent of the Christian youth would vote, the political landscape would change for the better. Politics is not a bad word. In simple terms, politics refers to governing or leading a group of people. Politics that once focused largely on the economy, national security, the deficit, and welfare, are now tackling important moral issues. These major issues have enormous implications. To remain silent actually makes a statement that we are not concerned enough. This is not just about the loss of jobs; it's about the loss of morality. We're not just talking about adding millions of dollars to the deficit; we're talking about aborting millions of babies. We're not only talking about providing housing for the poor; we're talking about creating life simply to destroy it. This shift requires Christians to stay closely involved.

Unfortunately, many do not see how apathy today will be our downfall tomorrow. Martin Luther King, Jr. said, "The church must be reminded that it is not the master or the servant of the state, but rather the conscience of the state ... If the church does not recapture its prophetic zeal, it will become an irrelevant social club without moral or spiritual

 Since evangelicals are often viewed as irrational and unintelligent, we need to engage the culture with wisdom, patience, discernment, and knowledge.

authority." What an insightful perspective, especially for us today.

The importance of government is irrefutable. Why would God ordain a government such as ours in America and then not want us to be involved? However, "extreme" demonstration and expression are often not the answer, nor is a total lack of interest—there must be a balance. The question shouldn't be, "Do we really think that we can make a difference?" but rather, "How can we make a difference according to the Scriptures?" I thank God for Christians who are involved and who influence America's political climate. I wish that there were more.

What can you do?

1. Lead a life of integrity regardless of what society promotes. Although only a select few can change government policy, all of us can build a life of moral integrity while staying committed to God's Word.

2. Pray and fast for our nation. **Prayer is more powerful than protest!** Pray specifically for more leaders guided by integrity. For those who doubt the power of prayer, consider this excerpt from the book, *One Nation Under God—The History of Prayer in America*: "prayer stands as one of the most critical and indisputable factors to have influenced the course of American history ... ."[53]

3. Vote for principles, not a particular party.

4. Become involved if God is calling you to that specific field of interest, but never initiate anything with a rebellious, prideful attitude—*you can be right in your reasoning, yet wrong in your attitude.* Since evangelicals are often viewed as irrational and

unintelligent, we need to engage the culture with wisdom, patience, discernment, and knowledge. Make sure that your actions are backed by a clear biblical mandate, and continually seek godly counsel.

5. Recognize diversity. Different people have different callings. God creates, within each of us, varying desires and levels of interests. If God has called a man to preach and teach His Word, that will be his passion. If God has called a Christian to pursue politics, that will be his passion, and so on. Problems arise when we fail to respect our differences. Activists should not expect everyone to share their passion for politics, and those who believe that Christians should stay out of politics must understand that not everyone agrees. God clearly calls some Christians to leadership.

6. Never give up. You can make a difference—we can make a difference. God will move mountains on behalf of one committed person. You might think that you are only one of a few in your community that is concerned about doing what is right. Elijah, an Old Testament prophet, felt the same way when he cried: *they have torn down Your altars and killed Your prophets, and only I am left.* But God responded, *I have seven thousand people that you do not know about who are still loyal to me* (I Kings 19). **Be encouraged … God simply asks that we do our part while He does His.**

Our only hope—it's not too late

In July 1776, during what many have called "one of the most historical events of all time," the Continental Congress of the United States of America officially declared independence, and its reputation as a great country was born.

America's patriots made tremendous sacrifices to secure liberty; we must make tremendous sacrifices to protect it.

Despite the beliefs of some, early Americans were not all renegades and rebels. For decades the Colonists tried to cooperate with England, but, as time passed, it became evident that change was needed. England needed to relinquish her oppressive, controlling grip. Although far from perfect, America's independence was built on the founding principles of life, liberty, and the pursuit of happiness.

Fortunately, there are many young adults from all cultures who are passionate about regaining lost ground. If you are one, I encourage you to follow this passion. America's patriots made tremendous sacrifices to secure liberty; we must make tremendous sacrifices to protect it.

At the beginning of this chapter, I included the last sentence of a famous quote often attributed to Alexis De Tocqueville. What I did not include was the rest of the quote. Paraphrasing, he stated that he looked throughout America to find where her greatness originated. He looked for it in her harbors and on her shorelines, in her fertile fields and boundless prairies, and in her gold mines and vast world commerce, but it was not there. He concluded with these words: "Not until I went to the churches of America and heard her pulpits aflame with righteousness did I understand the secret of her genius and power. America is great because she is good and if America ceases to be good, America will cease to be great."[54]

It's time to turn back to righteousness; back to the Bible; back to the proclamation of the gospel—America needs to repent and seek restoration. We should not apologize for preaching God's Word, redefine what He meant, or back down from conflict. **We are soldiers in the midst of a spiritual battle. We will be hated for following Christ, mocked for believing in truth, and challenged for promoting righteousness. We are called to deny ourselves, pick up our cross, and follow Him. Clearly, the day of the passive church is over.** We must lovingly preach righteousness in our pulpits again. The church should lead the fight (not against people), but against moral decline. "Righteousness exalts a nation, but sin is a reproach to any people" (Proverbs 14:34). Don't be fooled by thinking you can't make a difference—you can. Society changes as individuals change. As II Chronicles 7:14 so appropriately states: *if God's people will humble themselves and pray and seek His face and turn from their wicked ways, He will hear from heaven, forgive their sins, and heal their land.* **Without question, repentance, prayer, and humility before God is our only hope— it's not too late.**

Questions to consider for Chapter Eight:

1. Do you agree that it's important to understand why America was established? Is it also important to know just how far we have drifted off course? Why?

2. What was the intent of the Founders, and why did they believe it to be so important? Why is this truth being suppressed in our time? Why is it important

to remember what God did for America? (See
Deuteronomy 32:7.)

3. The State and the Church were to be separate in their
duties and functions, but interwoven in their core beliefs
and principles. How has the phrase "separation of
Church and State" been misapplied today?

4. America has been desensitized one generation at a
time, one court decision at a time, one compromise at a
time, and we are drowning in a cesspool of relativism.
How can we change this trend?

5. Name a few ways that you can be more involved in the
political process? Do you agree that remaining
silent actually makes a statement that you are not
concerned? Do you agree that it is time to turn back
to righteousness, back to the Bible, and back to the
proclamation of the gospel?

Recommended Reading:
Can God Bless America? by John MacArthur
Original Intent by David Barton
The Light and the Glory by Peter Marshall & David Manuel
America's Providential History by Mark A. Beliles & Stephen
K. McDowell
George Washington's Sacred Fire by Peter A. Lillback

For those interested, David Barton's book, *The Question of
Freemasonry and the Founding Fathers,* dispels the myth
that the Framers were influenced by Freemasonry. His
book, and many others, can be found at www.wallbuilders.
com. You may also consider visiting www.visionforum.com
for more helpful resources.

ABOUT THE AUTHOR

SHANE **I**DLEMAN'S PASSION FOR **G**OD'S **W**ORD MAY well have been planted nearly 400 years ago when the Pilgrims first set foot on American soil. Interestingly enough, Shane's maternal lineage can be traced to Peregrine White, the first baby born on the Mayflower in Cape Cod Bay. As the *Mayflower Compact* was signed, it's not unreasonable to believe that the signers committed America to God's guidance, and asked that their children and grandchildren would carry biblical principles into each generation. Shane not only believes that his passion may be in answer to that prayer spoken in the early hours of America's history, but he also believes that the spiritual baton is to pass from one generation to the next.

Today, as we continually drift away in a current of moral decline, many believe that the battle is too advanced and that we cannot make a difference. Shane, however, believes that we can, and offers this book as a contribution to that commitment.

Shane's ministry has sparked change in the lives of many. His bold stance has led to speaking engagements throughout the nation. He currently resides in Southern California.

BRACKETS SUCH AS THESE: [ ] were used when the author added his own thoughts to Scriptures or quotes. Not all famous quotes are referenced in the endnotes if the exact source could not be verified.

We've taken many avenues to make this book as comprehensive and complete as possible. However, as with any other book, there may be mistakes typographically and in subject matter. If you can identify any, we encourage you to contact us.

Scriptures and quotes within "quotation marks" are exact quotes; whereas paraphrased Scriptures and quotes are often *italicized*. In some cases, only portions of Scriptures are referenced; thus avoiding the need for ellipses in most cases. The Bible is the ultimate authority; all Scriptures should be read in their complete context whenever possible.

The New Strong's Expanded—exhaustive concordance of the Bible, © 2001, published by Thomas Nelson Publishers, was used to define words and meanings throughout the book.

All quotes from J.I. Packer can be found in his book, *Knowing and Doing the Will of God,* published by Random House Value Publishing, © 1995, 2000 by J.I. Packer.

1. D. James Kennedy, *The Silence of the Shepherds*, July 1997 issue of IMPACT; http://www.lex-rex.com/djk2.html.

2. Tozer, A.W., Book Two—*The Best of A.W. Tozer,* (used by permission of Christian Publications, Inc., www.christianpublications.com), p.49.

3. McDowell, Josh, *A Ready Defense*, (Thomas Nelson, Inc. © 1993), p.406.

4. Martin Luther, http://www.quoteworld.org (June 2004).

5. Tozer, *The Best of,* p.121.

6. Zacharias, Ravi, *Jesus Among Other God's,* (W Publishing Group, a Division of Thomas Nelson, Inc. © 2000), p.50.

7. Tozer, *The Best of,* p.116.

8. Martin, William C., *A Prophet With Honor—the Billy Graham Story,* (Quill, © 1991), p.63.

9. Tozer, A.W., *Rut, Rot or Revival,* (Christian Publications, Inc. © 1993), p.35.

10. Charles Haddon Spurgeon, *Sovereign Grace and Man's Responsibility*—sermon number 207 delivered August 1, 1858, at the Music Hall, Royal Surrey Gardens.

11. Used by permission of The CS Lewis Company Ltd; © CS Lewis Pte Ltd.

12. Charles Haddon Spurgeon, *The Holy Spirit's Chief Office*—sermon number 2382 delivered July 26th, 1888, at the Metropolitan Tabernacle, Newington.

13. Martin, *A Prophet With Honor,* pp.98-99.

14. "It's Almost Too Late," *New Man Magazine*—interview with Josh McDowell, May/June, 2003, p. 56.

15. Water, Mark, *Parallel Commentary on the New Testament*, p.63.

16. Chambers, Oswald, *The Complete Work of Oswald Chambers*, p.3.

17. Charles Haddon Spurgeon, *The Holy Spirit's Chief Office*—sermon number 2382 delivered on July 26th, 1888, at the Metropolitan Tabernacle, Newington.

18. Water, Mark, *Parallel Commentary on the New Testament—Spurgeon, Wesley, Henry,* (AMG Publishers, © 2003), p.741.

19. *Values Message Vanishes on Tube,* Los Angeles Daily News, November 22nd, 2004.

20. Charles R. Swindoll, August 2004 edition, *Insights* newsletter. Copyright © 2004. Published by Insight for Living, Plano, TX 75025, pp.1-2. (All rights reserved. Used by permission.) DOs and DON'Ts capitalized by author.

21. Tozer, A.W., Reprint from *The Root of the Righteous,* (used by permission of Christian Publications, Inc., www.christianpublications.com, © 1950, 1978, by Lowell Tozer), p. 5.

22. Chambers, Oswald, *The Complete Work of Oswald*

Chambers, (Published by Discovery House Publishers, © 2000, excerpt from *Approved unto God*), p.16.

23. Ibid, p.827. (Excerpt from September 27th; *My Utmost for His Highest.*)

24. Tozer, *The Best of,* p.67.

25. Chambers, *The Complete Work of Oswald Chambers*, p.762.

26. Swindoll, *Insights* newsletter, p.2.

27. Isaac Watts, *Abuses of the Emotions in Spiritual Life* (1746), quoted here from Mark A. Noll, *The Rise of Evangelicalism—the age of Edwards, Whitefield, and the Wesleys* (InterVarsity Press, © 2003), p.74.

28. Dobson, James, *Love for a Lifetime,* (Multnomah, © 1987, 1993, 1996, 1998), p.30.

29. "The Amputation Answer—Are you willing to do whatever is necessary to keep from falling into sin?," *New Man Magazine*, interview with Erwin Lutzer, March/April, 2004 (used by permission).

30. The author obtained this information from a message by Chip Ingram entitled, *Homosexuality: What Do You Say to Gay Friends?* This message can be found at www.lote.org.

31. Barnes, Craig, *Sacred Thirst;* Zondervan, © 2000; (used by permission of the Zondervan Corporation). Portion bolded by author.

32. For a list of some of these ingredients, see Ted Broer's book, *Maximum Energy,* (Siloam Press, © 1999).

33. John MacArthur, http://www.gty.org/bible_faqs, November, 2004.

34. Lyndon B. Johnson, *Public Papers of Presidents of the United States Containing the Public Messages, Speeches, and statements of the President* (Washington, DC: Government Printing Office, 1965), Book II: July 1 to December 31, 1964, p.884.

35. Chalfant, John W., *America—A Call To Greatness*, (America—A Call To Greatness, Inc. © 1996, 1999, 2003), p.9.

36. Barton, David, *The Role of Pastors & Christians in civil government,* (WallBuilders, Inc. © 2003), p.17. (Additionally, see Lutz, "Relative Influence," pp.191-193.)

37. Andrew Jackson, http://www.prayforleaders.org/quotes.html (2004).

38. D. James Kennedy, *Coral Ridge Ministries,* newsletter dated December 29th, 2003, p.1. (Additionally, see David Limbaugh's book, Persecution—in 1995 Samuel B. Kent, U.S. District judge for the Southern District of Texas, made this decree.)

39. Barton, *Original Intent*, p.12. (This quote is found in John Jay's will.)

40. Stone v. Graham, 449 U.S. 39 (1980). Additionally: Ring v. Grand Forks Public School District, 483 F. Supp. 272 (D.C. ND 1980).

41. Beliles & McDowell, *America's Providential History*, P.106.

42. Morris, B.F., *Christian Life and Character of the Civil Institutions of the United States*, (Philadelphia, 1864), p.234.

43. This quote by Washington cannot be documented, but there is overwhelming evidence to support that he held this belief. The second reference, "*Judge: Courthouse Bible Display Unconstitutional*," was posted at http://www.click2houston.com/news/3639446/detail.html, on August 10, 2004.

44. John Adams, *Works* (1856), Vol. X, p.45, to Thomas Jefferson on June 28th, 1813.

45. Beliles & McDowell, *America's Providential History*, P.184. Many acknowledge the fact that this quote is consistent with Henry's life and character even though it cannot be confirmed. It's possible that this unconfirmed quote came from Henry's uncle: Reverend Patrick Henry.

46. David Barton, http://www.wevotevalues.com/church_clips_info.html (October 22nd, 2004). Additionally, see Vidal v. Girard's Executors, 43 U. S. 126, 132 (1844).

47. Jefferson, *Writings*, Vol. XVI, pp.281-282, to the Danbury Baptist Association dated January 1, 1802. (See Barton, *Original Intent*, pp.43-48, for additional information.)

48. See Barton, *Original Intent*, pp.152-155, for additional information.

49. D. James Kennedy, *Special Report—Truth & Tyranny*, © 2003, p.1.

50. *People v. Ruggles*, 8 Johns 545 (Sup. Ct. NY. 1811).

51. D. James Kennedy, *The First Amendment on Trial*, June 2004, Coral Ridge Ministries Media newsletter, Inc., p.1, quoting Zell Miller in a Senate floor speech he presented on Feb. 12, 2004.

52. Used by permission of The CS Lewis Company Ltd; © CS Lewis Pte Ltd.

53. Moore, James P. Jr., *One Nation Under God—The History of Prayer in America*, (Doubleday, © 2005).

54. The quote, "*America is great because she is good...*", is commonly attributed to Alexis De Tocqueville; however, it is not found in his works. (For more information, refer to Beliles & McDowell, *America's Providential History*, P.116.)